MW01616471

MULTIPLY

WHAT THE BIBLE TEACHES ABOUT
SAVING, INVESTING, AND PLANNING
FOR YOUR FUTURE

TIM ROSEN

Copyright © 2019 by Tim Rosen. All Scripture quotations are taken from the King James Version. Special emphasis in verses is added.

All rights reserved. No part of this book may be reproduced, stored in a retrieval system, or transmitted in any form or by any means—electronic, mechanical, photocopy, recording, or otherwise—without written permission of the publisher, except for brief quotations in printed reviews.

Financial Compass Publications
815 W. Lancaster Blvd.
Lancaster, California 93534

The author and publication team have put forth every effort to give proper credit to quotes and thoughts that are not original with the author. It is not our intent to claim originality with any quote or thought that could not readily be tied to an original source.

ISBN 978-0-9829900-1-8

Printed in the United States of America

DEDICATION

To my wonderful wife of over thirty-one years, Victoria,
whose support and encouragement has made this
project possible.

CONTENTS

SHOULD CHRISTIANS SAVE FOR THEIR FINANCIAL FUTURE?

Scripture is rich in God's financial promises. He promises to feed and clothe those who seek first "…the kingdom of God, and his righteousness…" (Mathew 6:33), and He promises more than meeting the needs of those who honor Him in giving: "Honor the Lord with thy substance, and with the first fruits of all thine increase: So shall thy barns be filled with plenty, and thy presses shall burst out with new wine" (Proverbs 3:9–10).

The mistake many Christians make is hanging onto these promises of financial provision while giving ourselves a pass on how we manage the remainder of the money God has entrusted to us. We feel that as long as we give to the Lord, we can do as we please and spend as we wish. We do this to our detriment. God still calls us to be faithful stewards and His Word provides the wisdom for managing His resources. "Be thou diligent to know the state of thy flocks, and look well to thy herds" (Proverbs 27:23).

You may be thinking, "Hello, I don't have any flocks or herds!" Understand that Solomon gave us an illustration that his reading audience at the time would quickly relate to. Even as recent as the late 1700s, most Americans worked on farms. Knowing the state of your flock resonated as "keeping a sharp eye on your business!" Today, we would say, "Be diligent to know the state of your finances and look well to your dollars."

Fewer than half of Americans have calculated how much they need to save for retirement, and yet, the average American lives 20 years in retirement.[1] Twenty-nine percent of workers say they have less than $1,000 saved for retirement and 56% say the total value of investments is less than $25,000.[2]

There also exists the potential inability to work. An injury or illness can certainly derail our best-laid financial plans and cause a loss of income. Something as innocent as roughhousing and merely playing with your children can cause an injury that would put you out of work. I'm appealing to reason for proper planning—allowing for such possibilities.

A Disability Awareness study conducted in 2010 indicated that 64% of wage earners believe they have a 2% or less chance of being disabled for three months or more during

---

[1]   Source: U.S. Department of Labor
[2]   Source: Employee Benefits Research Institute, Retirement Confidence Survey, 2010c

their working career.[3] Whereas, the actual odds for a worker entering the workforce today are about 25%.[4]

"To feast now without regard to future famine is to manage our resources poorly and presume upon God or others to bail us out."—Randy Alcorn[5]

SAVING FOR A KNOWN, FUTURE NEED

Assumptions can get us all into a lot of trouble. When we are young, it's easy to assume that we have all the time in the world! When we are healthy and strong, it's easy to assume we'll always stay in such shape. When the paychecks are sizable, we assume the money will always be there.

Perhaps it's just easier for us to let assumptions take the place of real and responsible consideration and planning. There is a strange sense of *safety* living by certain assumptions and not asking ourselves and our spouses the hard and needed questions like, "How *should* we be eating to maintain good health?", "What steps should we be taking to remain valuable in our chosen careers?", and "How much money should we be setting aside for our future?"

Solomon holds no punches as he addresses the subject of saving, calling those who spend all their money *fools* and referring to those who save as *wise*. We find an admonition in

---

3   Council for Disability Awareness, Disability Divide Consumer Disability Awareness Study, 2010
4   U.S. Social Security Administration, Fact Sheet February 7, 2013,
5   Money, Possessions, and Eternity, Randy Alcorn, 1989, 2003 Eternal Perspectives Ministries, page 328

Proverbs 21:20, "There is treasure to be desired and oil in the dwelling of the wise; but a foolish man spendeth it up."

As long as we have breath, we will need income. "Go to the ant, thou sluggard; consider her ways, and be wise: Which having no guide, overseer, or ruler, Provideth her meat in the summer, and gathereth her food in the harvest" (Proverbs 6:6–8).

In teaching the wisdom of planning for a future need, our attention is drawn to the simplest of creatures who have no brain, yet they *prepare* for a future known need. We are called "sluggards," no doubt, to point out the need for us to plan, labor, and save for a known future need—yet many resist. Solomon did not claim that meat is easily provided for the ant. Instead, the ant has to go out and gather the meat for the present season as well as the coming season.

More than 21 million American workers expect to rely on Social Security in retirement, even though 56% admit to not having a good understanding of Social Security benefits. On average, these benefits equal 40% of one's salary. Is it anyone's goal to live off 40% of their pre-retirement income?

It's also important to consider the sustainability of the Social Security system, as it is currently administered. Thirty years ago (during the 1980s), there were slightly over 30 workers paying *into* Social Security for every one person *receiving* benefits. As of the writing of this book, there are presently less than three persons paying in for every one person drawing a benefit. What could it possibly look like 30 years from now?

The gap between what Social Security may pay, plus any pension you might be earning, and the actual amount you will need to live on, needs to be made up by your savings and investments. With today's low-interest rates, you will not be able to accumulate enough by savings alone. You will likely need to invest regularly so that your money can work harder for you and help you accumulate the funds you will need in the future.

Consider the source of your current income. There was action required on your part to attain it: education—perhaps earning a degree, applying for positions, presenting your worth and abilities in interviews, and when hired, working diligently. How should planning for our *future* income require any less effort?

Just as you plan and labor for your current source of income, so you ought to also plan and labor for your income later in life—it will not be simply handed to you.

"Man is ignorant of the future, but he must not allow his ignorance to make him so fearful that he becomes either careless or paralyzed. On the contrary, not knowing the future should make us more careful in what we plan and what we do."—Warren W. Wiersbe[6]

---

6   Be Satisfied, Warren W. Wiersbe. 2005, Cook Communications Ministries, page 12

INTRODUCTION

There is a threat looming over every adult today. I'm not talking about the dark, floating type that you would read about in a Frank Peretti novel. This is a threat that becomes stronger when we choose not to talk about it, or even acknowledge its existence. This threat is that one's cash flow would abruptly cease. No income, no employment, no disability benefits, nada. How can this happen? We keep living and aging, and at some point, are not able to continue earning our wages.

Is this cause for worry? No, worrying is not God's will for His children (Philippians 4:6). Is it cause for careful consideration and planning? Absolutely! Scripture is rich in principles and truths that we can and should apply to today's and tomorrow's finances. Saving and investing for a future known need is both wise and biblical.

Investing is an area that makes many people nervous, even fearful. But it doesn't have to when there are biblical principles we can learn and apply to our finances. While investing certainly provides the potential for the incredible growth of our assets, it also opens the doors to potential pitfalls, snares, and destruction. Infamous crimes such as the Bernie Madoff Ponzi scheme, which bilked investors out of more than $50 billion, have bred distrust toward money managers. Great drops in the markets of recent memory (2001, 2008) have struck fear into the hearts of many investors as well as would-be investors. And yet, we hear of others that are doing quite well in their investing endeavors.

Without discriminating, the investment world offers equal opportunities of either wealth creation, or obliteration; peace of mind, or panic. There are countless accounts of Christians losing wealth due to poor investment decisions, falling for scams or "get-rich-quick" plans, and being sold unsuitable investment products they don't understand.

How can you know which path is the right path? We live in a world with so much corruption that we often feel we cannot trust anyone. Where can you go to receive guidance that is actually in your best interest? The Bible. While today's terms and techniques may not be specifically mentioned in Scripture, the principles taught are timeless, relevant, and practical for today.

No economic crisis has ever taken God by surprise. Before the beginning of time, God already knew about every stock market crash, every era of poverty, and every season of economic depression. He didn't just know what would happen; He knew who would be affected. With a great love for all affected people, He imparted to holy men the wisdom necessary to deal with economic downfalls. That wisdom has been passed down to us through God's Word.

In Matthew 25, Jesus teaches that "...the kingdom of heaven is as a man traveling into a far country, who called his own servants, and delivered unto them his goods. And unto one he gave five talents, to another two, and to another one; to every man according to his several ability; and straightway took his journey. Then he that had received the five talents went and traded with the same and made them other five talents" (vs. 14-16). The parable teaches us that we are to be faithful stewards of all that God has entrusted us with and occupy until He returns, and increase, or further, the kingdom of heaven.

When I look at verse fourteen, I can't help but think, "How did this servant double his master's wealth in only one verse?" Apparently, the length of a verse does not correlate to the amount of time and effort these servants invested into increasing their master's wealth. But it got me thinking, *what would have been the first steps that these faithful servants took the moment they received such great wealth?*

Did they seek advice? Were they just lucky? Did they make mistakes? Did they worry or fret over such responsibility?

What Scripture would have been complete at that time, and available to these first-century servants, from which to seek wisdom and guidance?

Join me as we *step into the sandals* of these faithful servants and learn what they may have learned, read the Scripture they may have read, seek the counsel they may have sought, and avoid the pitfalls they may have avoided, all in an effort to increase what had been entrusted to their care.

CHAPTER ONE

REMEMBER WHO THE OWNER IS

For the kingdom of heaven is as a man travelling into a far country, who called his own servants, and delivered unto them his goods.

Matthew 25:14

MULTIPLY

Yada's servants had been serving him for varying periods of time. Some only recently came under the service and employment of this great man, while others had grown up in his household. None will forget that hot summer morning when they were all summoned to the front courtyard. "The lord demands your presence in the courtyard at once!" bellowed the stone-faced sentry.

As they hastily came to attention, standing side by side under the unmerciful sun, it became quite clear that their master was prepared to travel. Judging by the number of camels, horses and carts assembled, along with a dozen soldiers, Abdiel quickly surmised that this was to be a journey unlike any other in the past. Their master seemed ready to travel for an indefinite period of time.

Abdiel struggled to keep his usual, pleasant and ready countenance. Inwardly, he fought back an overwhelming sense of despondency—he had lived with this dear man since childhood and could not imagine what his life would be like without him.

With great interest, he watched as the master of the house and his treasurer approached, carrying bags weighted down with what must be gold. Now, Abdiel's mind was racing...

Why is he bringing his gold over to his servants?

Doesn't he need his gold for his journey?

AS THESE SERVANTS WATCHED their lord prepare to leave for his journey, they were keenly aware that the wealth being handed to them was not theirs to do with as they pleased, but was the property of their master, and they had the responsibility of managing that wealth in his absence.

Our Lord ascended into heaven forty days after His resurrection, with the promise that He is going to prepare a place for us, and that He will return to receive us unto Himself, that we may always be with Him. He did not give us the date of His return. He expects that we should trust and live faithfully for Him until He returns, "Occupy till I come." What does occupying look like?

Living in a physical world, we naturally look around and view many things as "ours." This is our house, our car, our dog, our collectible coffee mugs—you can continue the list. While we may be willing to share many of these items, it gets really personal when it comes to money. Our money is not something we readily talk about with others. Can you imagine talking about money as casually as we do family, work, and fun?

"Hey Scott! How have you been?"

"Oh fine, had a great time at the Lake. The kids got over their colds, and I still have $2,317 in the bank."

That doesn't really happen, does it?

Talking about money seems to be taboo or relegated to those who enjoy boasting—so we simply do not talk about it. Oftentimes, this carries over into marriages where husbands and wives avoid the serious conversations about money. We fumble in our conversations about money because of our perceptions. We regard money as a private matter and perceive ourselves as the absolute owner of all we possess. In reality, God is the absolute owner of all things. First Corinthians 10:26 says, "For the earth is the Lord's and the fullness thereof."

Everything belongs to God. All that we have comes from the Lord. James 1:17 teaches us that, "Every good gift and every perfect gift is from above, and cometh down from the Father of lights, with whom is no variableness, neither shadow of turning."

While we are given great latitude with how we can use the great resources God entrusts us with, we must remember that we are the stewards of His resources. The American Heritage Dictionary defines a steward as "one who manages another's property, finances, or other affairs." In today's vernacular, we would say, a manager. As managers, we are put in charge of the care and oversight of the resources belonging to God, placed in our trust.

God is very interested in what we do with His resources, and we must remember that the number one reason we are all here on this earth is to give glory to God and to honor Him in all we do.

We are admonished in Colossians 3:17, "And whatsoever ye do in word or deed, do all in the name of the Lord Jesus, giving thanks to God and the father by him."

GOD'S ASSETS: ENTRUSTED TO OUR MANAGEMENT AND FOR HIS GLORY

Our view of the one who owns the money we manage greatly impacts how we handle that money. If we view money as something we own outright, we will then utilize it for our own purposes and pleasures. Our own purposes and pleasures are highly weighted toward the temporal. There are physical needs in this life that need to be met, along with plenty of wants and desires that require money. But if we look and operate through the temporal lens, we are going to experience results of the temporal. These include:

✕ **Worry over having enough money to take care of ourselves and our families** (Jesus said in Matthew 6:32a, "For after all these things do the Gentiles seek.")

✕ Trusting in the balance of our savings or investments. "Charge them that are rich in this world, that they be not highminded, nor *trust in uncertain riches*, but in the living God, who giveth us richly all things to enjoy" (1 Timothy 6:17).

✕ **Having more than enough with seemingly no needs, which leads us (even unsuspectingly) to "…** be full, and deny thee, and say, Who is the Lord?" (Proverbs 30:9)

✕ **Loving money and the things that money brings, more than we love God.** "For the love of money is the root of all evil: which while some coveted after,

*they have erred from the faith, and pierced themselves
through with many sorrows"* (1 Timothy 6:10).

× **Pain for ourselves and our families.** "But they that
will (to desire) be rich fall into temptation and a snare,
and into many foolish and hurtful lusts, which drown
men in destruction and perdition" (1 Timothy 6:9).

However, if we view money and possessions by faith,
through the eternal lens of Scripture, we can avoid this turmoil.
We learn in God's Word that God not only owns the earth "…
and the fullness thereof," but also "the world, and they that
dwell therein" (Psalm 24:1). He owns *us*.

Yes, the God of the universe—the One who spoke the
heavens and earth into existence in just six days, who knew
our days before we had any, and punished His own Son for
our sins—owns our lives, in their *entirety*. First Corinthians
6:19-20 declares, "What? Know ye not that your body is the
temple of the Holy Ghost which is in you, which ye have
of God, *and ye are not your own? For ye are bought with a
price*: therefore glorify God in your body, and in your spirit,
which are God's." This passage uses explicit language: "ye are
not your own"—"bought with a price"—"body, and…spirit,
which are God's." The wonderful truth is, since God owns
us, He owns our cares and burdens! We don't have to carry
burdens (including financial burdens) because they belong to
God; cast them upon Him (1 Peter 5:7).

Knowing that God is the true owner who carries our burdens, we can be free of money-related stress, worry, fear, doubt, and covetousness. Think about that! Why worry over something that is not yours? All is His. The *owner* bears the burden of ownership, not the *manager* or *steward*. Our job is to faithfully and wisely manage what the owner has entrusted to us.

According to Scripture, God equips us with all the resources we need. But what exactly are we equipped for? God gives us promises of provision and blessings in finances so that we may be equipped "…to every good work" (2 Corinthians 9:8).

Therein lies the key: "*every good work.*" What is a good work? Everything God's Word instructs us to do: reach the lost (Matthew 28:19–20), provide for our families (1 Timothy 5:8), support our pastor (1 Timothy 5:17), save for our future income needs (Proverbs 6:6; Proverbs 21:20), help our brothers and sisters-in-Christ (Galatians 6:10), and show God's love to the poor (Proverbs 3:27–28; 1 John 3:17).

I want to challenge you in the following chapters, to approach money and investing as the manager of God's resources, rather than the owner.

🖋 PUTTING IT INTO PRACTICE

The Owner bears the burden. What burdens have you been carrying, as an owner rather than steward, that you need to give to the Lord? Write them here:

_____

_____

_____

_____

_____

_____

_____

_____

Viewing yourself as the Manager of the financial resources that God has entrusted to you, what changes would you need to make in order to honor the Lord in your finances?

_____

_____

_____

_____

_____

_____

_____

_____

CHAPTER TWO

VARYING GIFTS, VARYING ABILITIES

And unto one he gave five talents, to another two,
and to another one; to every man according to his
several ability; and straightway took his journey.

Matthew 25:15

"Abdiel, you have accomplished much in your service to me and have demonstrated diligence and wisdom. I am entrusting you with five talents. Increase this wealth with wisdom and enterprise."

Abdiel almost fell to his knees, overwhelmed with gratitude and humility.

"Thank you, my lord, I will not disappoint you!"

"Bartel," their master said to the second servant, "you have shown yourself dependable and resourceful as well. Take these two talents and multiply them for me."

"Thank you, my lord," said Bartel.

"Taneli..." he said to the third and last servant. Taneli was looking down with his chin to his chest.

"Taneli, look at me..." said his master, while gently lifting Taneli's face. He looked deep into Taneli's eyes and paused until he had his full attention.

"Take this talent and be diligent to increase its worth. I will return."

"Yes, my lord," Taneli replied.

With that, their lord turned and departed. Abdiel and Bartel stood and watched their lord until all they could see were dust clouds on the horizon. Taneli promptly returned to his own chambers.

WE SEE THAT THEIR LORD distributed his wealth to each servant according to the faithfulness they have previously displayed. We also see that he extended grace by giving a portion to his servant that had not demonstrated faithfulness while in his employ. He gave him another opportunity to be faithful in his absence.

Christians are not going to have the same amount of money as each other. We will not have the same quality cars, houses, or leisure time. That's okay. God has a unique plan for your life. Your life is not intended to be a replica of someone else's. The stewards in this parable, no doubt, compared the wealth given to each of them and this may have aroused jealousy, gossip, and anger.

The Apostle Paul teaches that it is not wise for us to compare ourselves with each other (2 Corinthians 10:12).

God knows our individual strengths and weaknesses. Thankfully, He is very patient with us and allows us time to grow in our Christian walk. We all have areas in our lives that we desire to improve on. You may look back and recall specific areas in your own life where you've grown by God's grace. You might be a little more patient now than you used to be. Perhaps you are more empathetic to the hurts of others than you were previously. The wonderful truth is that God is not done working on us—molding us to be more like Him.

God gives us opportunities and resources *now*—according to our current faithfulness and trustworthiness. As we grow and improve our faithfulness, He will multiply our opportunities and increase our financial resources so that we make a greater impact on eternity.

God has called all of His children to be faithful stewards in every area that He has entrusted us with (1 Corinthians 4:2). Just a few areas we are to be faithful and careful are our health, time, family, the Gospel, and our finances

> He that is faithful in that which is least is faithful also in much: and he that is unjust in the least is unjust also in much. (Luke 16:10)

Are we faithful with all that the Lord has currently entrusted us with? I'm sure we all feel that we can do better. We can be more *faithful in that which is least* so that we can be faithful with more. I believe one of the greatest hindrances to our efforts in financial faithfulness is worry and fear.

In Matthew chapter six, Jesus speaks at length addressing our tendency to worry about physical needs. We worry about what we are going to eat, what we are going to wear, where we are going to live, where we are going to work—the list goes on.

Then Jesus seems to shake us to get our attention, as if to say, "Look at me. Stop worrying. What are these things that you are concerned about? Those are the things the unbelievers worry about. You do not need to worry. Look at the birds. They don't have to apply for jobs, pay bills, or wonder how they are going to make it. I take care of them! And you are much more valuable to me than birds!" (See Matthew 6:26)

Then we see the promise, "…and all these things (food, clothing, shelter) shall be added unto you." But, there is a condition. Action is required on our part, "But seek ye first the kingdom of God, and his righteousness" (Matthew 6:33). Are we first seeking His kingdom? Do we love His appearing? Do we seek daily, even by the hour, to live righteously? We receive His promised provision only when we do those things.

> For the LORD God is a sun and a shield: the LORD will give grace and glory: no good thing will he withhold from them that walk uprightly. (Psalm 84:11)

If we desire to have more so that we can *do* more (give, save, invest), then the starting point is faithful stewardship now.

WHAT DOES FAITHFULNESS IN OUR FINANCES LOOK LIKE TODAY?

The heart that desires to cheerfully honor the Lord in finances, finds that God blesses that desire.

"There is that scattereth and yet increaseth" (Proverbs 11:24a).

"…and he which soweth bountifully shall reap also bountifully" (2 Corinthians 9:6b).

God works through His children to further the kingdom through giving: supporting missionaries, giving to building programs, special offerings, and helping the poor. Jesus assures us that we are storing up for ourselves treasures in heaven when we give to kingdom purposes. These treasures will last for all eternity without being taxed, stolen, or eroded by inflation, which is essentially what Matthew 6:20 says.

There will be no regret for our sacrificial giving during this short lifetime when we get to our eternal home in the world to come.

BEING DILIGENT WITH DOLLARS

We have expenses in life after honoring the Lord with our tithes and offerings. You know these all too well: housing costs, utility bills, groceries, and insurance. It is interesting to consider all the things we would label as *needs* today. If we look at the previous generation's needs, we will not find internet service, smartphones, tablets, streaming TV service, or cloud storage on the list. Chances are that we would find "retirement contributions" on their list of needs.

The past generation witnessed the dissolving of the company pension plan and the shift in focus to the 401(k) as a means of retirement planning. Today, we are both blessed and challenged with innovation. On the one hand, there are many time-saving tools and applications at our disposal, while on the other hand, there is a strong cultural emphasis on consuming entertainment and enjoyment.

We add monthly subscriptions and the purchase of devices by convincing ourselves that they are needs. Now, I am not against innovations and technology—I'm a huge proponent. But I do observe that there is more and more emphasis on consumerism and entertainment today that effectively distracts us from planning for tomorrow. Solomon wrote, "Be thou diligent to know the state of thy flocks and look well to thy herds" (Proverbs 27:23).

We can follow a biblical pattern of honoring the Lord (Proverbs 3:9–10), saving, investing a portion for ourselves (Proverbs 21:20, Proverbs 6:6), and paying for our costs of living (2 Corinthians 9:8) with today's income.

▤ PUTTING IT INTO PRACTICE

Solomon instructs us to know the state our wealth; our bank accounts, investments, and dollars. Are you confident in knowing where all your dollars are going? Are there areas where you can improve efficiency?

_____

_____

_____

_____

_____

_____

_____

Exercise: Review your two months of bank statements. Look through each transaction. In what categories (i.e shopping, dining out, entertainment) can you reduce your monthly expenditures?

_____

_____

_____

_____

_____

_____

By what amount can you reduce spending in these categories and still meet your needs?

_____

_____

_____

_____

_____

_____

_____

_____

_____

Add up the dollars that you have identified, that can be redirected to savings and investing. Write that amount here:

_____

_____

_____

_____

_____

_____

_____

_____

_____

CHAPTER THREE

CLARIFY YOUR PURPOSE FOR INVESTING

Then he that had received the five talents went
and traded with the same...

Matthew 25:16

MULTIPLY

Abdiel felt a renewed sense of loyalty. He was determined to make his lord proud of him. He purposed in his heart and mind not to disappoint his master. He will commit to multiplying his lord's wealth entrusted to his care. He would need to put this money to work, to increase its value so that one day, he would be able to present to his master an impressive sum!

AS FOR THE FAITHFUL SERVANTS, they were tasked to greatly increase the value of the wealth that was entrusted to them, thus pleasing their lord.

What is your motivation to save and invest? Can you clearly state to a young person what your specific, measurable goal is? If we have not clearly defined our personal purpose for saving and investing, no matter how much we accumulate, enough will never seem to be enough. Without a clear goal, the answer to the question, "How much is enough?" will always be, "More." Without purpose, the pursuit of wealth is empty and meaningless.

There are those who easily get nervous or anxious when they do not know if they are on track to have enough money for their future. They may worry that what they are currently doing is *not enough*. Then there are those who have more than enough for now as well as for their future, but still feel unfulfilled.

Solomon warned, "He that loveth silver shall not be satisfied with silver; nor he that loveth abundance with increase: this also is vanity" (Ecclesiastes 5:10).

Through our tithes and offerings, we increase our Lord's kingdom. Through saving and investing, we prepare for a known future need in our lives, should the Lord tarry His coming.

Most investors have a general idea as to why they want to invest. In many cases, it is for retirement income. According to a recent Fox poll, nearly 88% of people say that retirement is a top priority.[1] For some, it is to pay for their children's college education, or even a wedding or two. With that goal in mind, how much money will that goal require? How much time do you have before that money is needed? Knowing the future approximate dollar amount needed will help you know how much to invest each month to reach that goal.

SAVING AND INVESTING FOR A LARGE PURCHASE

The purchase of a home, a car, and even a wedding are considered a "Big-ticket item," and it can be paid for through our saving efforts. When you wish to save for a big-ticket item and have fewer years to do so; it is wise to make monthly deposits into a savings account rather than investing in the stock market. No, you will not earn much interest. But the priority is that your money is accessible and will be there for you without fluctuating in value.

A helpful axiom is, "Save for the short-term goals, invest for the long-term goals."

INVESTING FOR FUTURE INCOME

For many, investing is the necessary means to accumulate enough money to create an income during retirement years. This can be a wise and worthy pursuit, depending on age and amount of time before the desired retirement date.

---

1   https://www.foxnews.com/politics/fox-news-poll-the-american-dream

If retirement income is the purpose of investing, what goal do we aim for? How do we know how much money is required? Is it even possible?

Let's look at some simple guidelines in determining how much money is needed to generate a future income. In the pages that follow, we will learn the biblical principles to apply to the *process* of saving and investing.

DETERMINING HOW MUCH IS NEEDED TO CREATE YOUR FUTURE INCOME.

Begin with the end in mind. "Better is the end of a thing than the beginning thereof" (Ecclesiastes 7:8).

Let's use the example of $45,000 as a desired future income. Let's also account for a Social Security benefit (whether two persons are receiving benefits or one) of $2,000 per month which is $24,000 per year. The difference that we need to make up for is $21,000 per year.

> ### NOTE
>
> If you have been paying into Social Security and anticipate retirement benefits, visit www.ssa.gov. There you can register and view your future benefits online. You will notice varying benefit amounts depending on your age when you choose to start your monthly benefits. You can factor in those dollar amounts to help determine how much additional income you will need in order to live comfortably.

How much do we need to accumulate throughout our working years in order to generate the additional annual income of $21,000?

To answer this, let's start by fast-forwarding to your hypothetical retirement date. You've disciplined yourself by investing every month (or every paycheck) throughout your working career, and now, you have a *nest-egg* of $600,000 - (which is very feasible). If you happen to be about age 65, you might want to plan your finances allowing for 20-25 years of living in retirement or longer. To make your money last that long while drawing an income, most financial experts agree that you can withdraw 4.0% of your balance as income—from a prudently allocated portfolio (we'll cover diversification and allocation in chapter 6).

By taking your *future* balance and multiplying by .04, you can get an idea of the income that can be drawn, intended to last the rest of your life. Withdrawing .04 of $600,000 is $24,000, or more than enough to meet your needed future income. Investing more dollars per month, during your working years, and given more time, you can accumulate a higher balance so that you can withdraw a larger future income in order to keep up with inflation.

Example: Withdrawing 4% annually from an $800,000 balance is $32,000 per year compared to $24,000 from a $600,000 balance.

THE COST OF LIVING INCREASES OVER TIME

We should expect that ten years from now, groceries will cost more than they do today. Fuel, vehicle prices, taxes, and utilities all increase over time. So, if we are currently able to live off an income of $45,000 for example, that same $45,000 ten years from now will not buy as much as it does today. It may require $60,000, ten years from now, to maintain your current lifestyle—and we should plan for that increase.

If we use 3% as the average increase in the price of goods and services, we can expect our cost of living (groceries, utilities, and clothing for example) in ten years to be about 34% higher than it is today! (3% per year compounded annually).

The farther away our potential retirement year is from now, the more we should account for the cost of living to increase.

I remember the first new sedan I bought in 1990 out of necessity—my family had grown by one person, my baby boy, and we needed the extra room. The purchase price was $13,000. Ten years later, I bought a replacement sedan, modest, and in the same category, and its price tag was $21,000. I drove that thing into the ground within a short period and needed a replacement car six years later. The price tag of the new modest sedan? $33,000!

While I may have and should have shopped for used cars, as I do now, the reality is, the costs of durable goods increase over time. It is wise to factor this into our savings and invest for our future needs.

It's reasonable to consider that by retirement, certain bills and expenses may be eliminated, such as child-raising related expenses, vehicles are hopefully paid for, and many will have paid their mortgages off. If you are on such a path, then your future income may not need to be as high as we are projecting here.

HEALTH INSURANCE

In recent years, many Americans have witnessed the cost of their health insurance increase sharply. For my family, it seems to be increasing every three months or so. Some have had their costs doubled, some tripled.

What we can account for is that health insurance coverage is costly, especially if you have to pay the full amount yourself, not having coverage through an employer or as part of your retirement benefits package. It is important to plan so that we can continue to pay for health insurance during our retirement years. A small percentage of workers today will continue to be covered with health insurance as an employee benefit from their employer—that is a huge blessing. It is a good idea to check with the benefits department of your employer to review your future retirement benefits (if any) to help you plan accordingly.

Medicare does provide a level of coverage for those who: (a) have paid into the system, and (b) have reached age 65. It is costly to be unhealthy. The ten-year mean for medical costs for obesity ranges from $33,010 to $40,873.[2] The personal costs per person with Diabetes averages $11,700 per year.[3]

We should plan for the monthly costs of health insurance to increase over time. Through prudent investing, it is possible to accumulate the funds necessary to pay this bill, and other living expenses, in the future.

2   http://endocrinefacts.org/health-conditions/obesity/ Last viewed
    October 7, 2018
3   http://endocrinefacts.org/health-conditions/diabetes-2/   Last view
    February 7, 2017

📝 PUTTING IT INTO PRACTICE

What is important to you about money, something that is a bigger issue than the money itself?

_____

_____

_____

_____

_____

_____

_____

_____

Could you distill that down to just one word? (For example, Love, Family, Helping, Livelihood).

_____

_____

_____

_____

_____

_____

_____

_____

What is your accumulation goal? (This figure can adjust over time. It is important to have a starting point).

_____

_____

_____

_____

_____

_____

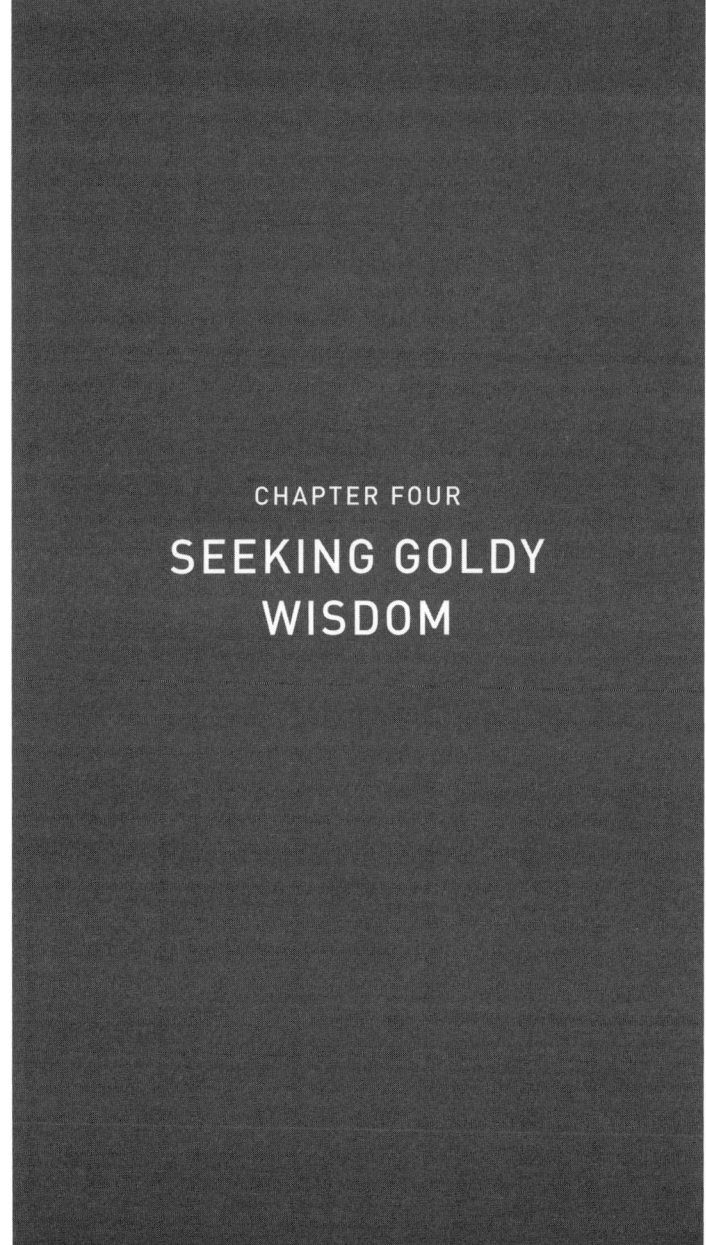

CHAPTER FOUR

SEEKING GOLDY WISDOM

MULTIPLY

Abdiel delayed not in his giving thanks to God for this blessing and privilege. In his prayer closet, he bowed and worshipped the God of Abraham, Isaac, and Jacob. He confessed that this undertaking is greater than him—he needed God's wisdom and guidance.

He arose and washed himself, then entered the room where his lord kept the sacred books of Scripture and carefully lifted the book of the Proverbs. He purposed to commit an hour of reading and studying before resuming his daily responsibilities on the grounds. Tomorrow, he would seek an audience with Caleb, a merchant who fears the LORD and has been diligent in business as long as Abdiel can remember. Perhaps Caleb will be willing to provide some guidance and direction in this new undertaking.

ROB IS A SENIOR SAINT in our church whose wife of many years recently passed away. A few months after her passing, Rob approached me and asked for my input on his finances. In just a few short minutes, I had learned that Rob had trusted a broker, the brother-in-law of a church member, with his retirement account, and according to Rob, "he assured me that he could make a lot of money for me investing my savings of $170,000."

He was never informed as to the plans of this stockbroker, but judging by his statements, there were excessive buying and selling transactions and even some options trading which Rob didn't understand. Several years later, as the broker's marriage fell apart and he quit the business, he couldn't be found; phones were disconnected, and the office space was empty. Rob called the corporate office to ask about what happened to his money and heard, "Wow! Yea, that account really took a bite!" His $170,000 had been traded and speculated with, realizing losses of over $125,000, leaving Rob (retired and living in a trailer), with $45,000. It's hard to say if this situation was completely avoidable, but I do know that Rob did not seek counsel. Had he sought his Pastor for counsel, letting him know that he was considering investing with this man, he could have learned that this broker had speculated with other church members' investments and tends to favor riskier investments such as trading options.

> Where no counsel is, the people fall: but in the multitude of counsellors there is safety. (Proverbs 11:14)

God has provided a multitude of counselors, and sources of counsel, to help guide us. Let's look at a few:

THE BIBLE

We read the Bible to learn about God. We go to the Bible to find His plan for salvation through His Son, Jesus Christ. Many of us search through Psalms for comfort, Ephesians for spiritual armor, and Philippians to learn how to be more like Christ. It is through God's Word that we are introduced to faith, and also learn to pray. Yet the subject of money has twice as many verses dedicated to it than faith and prayer combined.

That might sound strange at first, and it could be due to our own perceptions of money; we may not view money as a spiritual topic—certainly not one requiring so much scripture. While money is indeed important to *us*, it may be that we prefer not to have the light of Scripture shining on our financial practices. How often, if at all, do we turn to the Bible for financial counsel?

The wonderful thing is, our Master has given us the Bible, rich in truth and wisdom, and we can learn *how* to be that faithful servant by reading and applying its principles. For example, we can learn from reading Proverbs that we don't have to be in a rush in our efforts to save and invest. We can, instead, focus on being faithful and enjoy God's blessings: "A faithful man shall abound with blessings: but he that maketh haste to be rich shall not be innocent" (Proverbs 28:20).

Solomon, the human author of most of the Proverbs, also teaches the wisdom of having savings (Proverbs 21:20;

Proverbs 6:6), the principle of diversification (Ecclesiastes 11:1), and warns against indebtedness (Proverbs 22:7).

The Bible contains many Parables that Jesus taught, using elements (like money) that we all would readily understand. Of all the parables which Jesus taught, sixteen were lessons related to finances. He taught with an emphasis on our hearts toward money. He also helps us to learn what *true* riches are, by charging us to transfer our temporal wealth to our heavenly home, where it will last for eternity (Matthew 6:20).

Paul teaches us the promise of God to those who give, that God will feed them, continue to provide for them to give, and increase the fruits of their giving (2 Corinthians 9:10). He warns Christians of the great destruction that comes into the life of the one who loves money (1 Timothy 6:9–10), and challenges us in word and deed, to learn to be content (Philippians 4:11–12).

From the books of Moses to Psalms and Proverbs, Ecclesiastes to the Gospels and Epistles, there are over 2,300 verses from which to learn the mind of Christ in this matter of money. It is not God's design that we rely on our wisdom to figure out financial issues, but that we search His Word for guidance. He has provided a wealth of counseling on the subject, and it is worthy of our time and effort to seek it out.

The Psalmist knew well the counsel that the Scripture provided when he wrote, Thy testimonies also are my delight and my counsellors (Psalm 119:24).

As you read through the Bible, why not have a highlighter pen with you, and every time you read a portion of Scripture that speaks to the subject of money, riches, giving or possessions, highlight those verses, then prayerfully consider how God would have you to apply those truths to your life. These biblical principles will be our guide throughout this book.

GODLY COUNSELLORS

It is both wise and profitable to seek counsel from godly men or woman whom you respect. Proverbs 15:22 reminds us, "Without counsel purposes are disappointed: but in the multitude of counsellors they are established."

Can you remember times in your life when you were so excited about a new undertaking that you jumped in, having great expectations, only to be disappointed that your expectations were not met? Investing is undoubtedly one of those endeavors that I continue to hear story after story of unmet expectations. Even beyond unmet expectations are stories of hurt, loss, and pain. When I dig deeper into those stories, I find a common cause: lack of proper counsel, or flat out *bad* counsel.

King Rehoboam sought counsel, and there was no lack of persons more than willing to advise the new king. He first heard from *the old men who stood with his father Solomon*, and then he heard from his buddies. If it were you, whose advice would you take? The advice from men who stood with, spent time with, and even counseled with the wisest man to ever live? Or your buddies? Of course, hindsight makes us all look like geniuses, "Listen to Solomon's men!" But under peer pressure, and even having your ego stroked a bit; it's not hard to make the wrong choice. And that's exactly what Rehoboam did. Rather than extending grace to the children of Israel, as recommended by the *old men*, Rehoboam chose to take his friends' advice and afflict the children of Israel even more than they were already suffering. He made an unwise choice, followed the wrong counsel, and it did not please God. Rehoboam's life and his kingdom did not end well.

Brothers and sisters-in-Christ, who are older than us, can be a great source for seeking counsel—though keep in mind, age itself is not a qualifier—I have counseled many couples older than I and have had to teach them how to *start* handling their finances diligently. A godly walk, age, experience, and a *good name* are all attributes to look for when seeking counsel from another person whom you respect.

PROFESSIONALS WITH A GOOD NAME.

"A good name is rather to be chosen than great riches…" (Proverbs 22:1). I used to change my car's oil myself. When I owned a 1970 Ford Mustang, it was easy to work on, as far as changing the oil and filters. I could not service the transmission nor the engine; I did not have the training or expertise. Have you looked under the hood of a recently manufactured car? You can't see any moving parts! It's all computers, and the engine is covered over with plastic shields; the only maintenance work I can perform today is to put gas in the tank, check the tire pressure, and refill the windshield wiper fluid.

The systems in today's vehicles are complicated. Thankfully, there are trained, certified mechanics who can service my vehicle when the need arises. I don't take my car to just anyone; I've found a mechanic who is competent, has a good name in our community, and has *shown* himself to be honest. It helps me to have confidence and peace of mind, knowing I have the right person for the job.

The same is true with our finances. We want an expert to advise and help us with our investing. Someone who is competent, honest, and has a *good name* in his industry. There are several ways to research a financial professional before visiting him or her.

One way is to simply ask your friends, family, fellow church members, if they know this person and know of their work. Second would be to search their "online" reputation.

Through Google or another online search engine, you can type this person's name in, along with their city and state and quite often find the answers to many of your questions. With the World Wide Web, it has become all but impossible to hide anything—people will share their experiences, good or bad, online for others to see (Yelp! For instance, offers public reviews of restaurants and service organizations) Today, the consumer is very willing to share their experiences, so that others may either be motivated or warned.

What are people saying about the particular professional you are researching? Are there legitimate complaints or concerns posted? These could help you avoid a potentially harmful experience. It's important to note that the law prohibits investment advisors from using client testimonials, so you will not likely find the *praises* of a person of interest listed online. It is best to speak with people who are currently using or have used their services. Are they pleased with this professional? Would they highly recommend you do business with them?

It is essential to learn what services a professional is licensed to offer and the source of their compensation. Are they licensed to sell insurance, mutual funds, stocks and bonds for a commission? Or are they licensed to advise for a fee? There is a huge difference.

Financial professionals, like all people, have temptations to battle. Whether it is a desire to grow their business or the drive to succeed, brokers may be motivated by a big paycheck from their commission ahead of (or at least in addition to) offering a solution that is best for the client without the commission that would be taken from the client's pocket.

With fee-based advisors, the pressure to "close the sale" is greatly reduced, or even eliminated. Advisors who are free from the need to sell can serve the client without a hidden agenda.

VERIFY

On December 8, 1987, President Reagan and Mikhail Gorbachev signed the Intermediate-Range Nuclear Forces Treaty (INF) which would "eliminate and permanently forswear all of their nuclear and conventional ground-launched ballistic and cruise missiles with ranges of 500 to 5,500 kilometers."[1] This treaty

---

1   https://www.armscontrol.org/factsheets/INFtreaty

was crucial in putting an end to the Cold War between these two superpowers. As they appeared before the cameras, and millions of viewers, President Reagan, with his famous grin, quoted a Russian proverb to Mikhail Gorbachev, "doveryai no proveryai. Trust but verify." Mr. Gorbachev chuckled and said (translated in English), "You always say that!"

"I like it," President Reagan replied. I like it also, trust but verify.

According to a study prepared for the Financial Industry Regulatory Authority Investor Education Foundation, 84% of Americans have been solicited with a potentially fraudulent investment offer. According to the FBI, nearly $40 Billion every year is lost due to investment fraud.[2]

"All healthy humans are vulnerable to fraud," writes Pat Huddleston in his book, *The Vigilant Investor* [2011]. This does not mean we should be fearful of investing. Christians do not have to be *vulnerable*; we should be vigilant. I like that word. It means to be careful, watchful. The prospect of investing is worthy of being careful and doing some homework. The Bible teaches us, "He that getteth wisdom loveth his own soul: he that keepeth understanding shall find good" (Proverbs 19:8).

The first step in avoiding fraud is to understand that fraud can be all around you. The second step is to choose one investing professional to guide you. The vigilant investor favors investment advisors who get a vigilant, independent audit of all funds in which they invest. Which brings us to the third step: verify.

---

2   Huddleston, Pat, The Vigilant Investor, AMACOM (October 25, 2011)

The vigilant investor should take this a step further; they should verify, then trust! If investments are being recommended and "historical rates of return" are being touted, ask for an audited returns report—anyone can throw out big numbers in hopes of impressing or convincing the potential investor to invest his or her wealth. If they stutter or fumble at that request, maybe it's time to move on to the next potential advisor.

"Through wisdom is an house built; and by understanding it is established: And by knowledge shall the chambers be filled with all precious and pleasant riches" (Proverbs 24:3–4).

📝 PUTTING IT INTO PRACTICE

Take a few moments and think about three people who you would identify as wise, mature, and financially responsible. Write their names below.

_____

_____

_____

_____

_____

_____

_____

Now, of these three, which one would you hand over the keys to your house while you are away for six months? (This part is hypothetical). Write this person's name, as this is the one you trust the most.

_____

_____

_____

_____

_____

After completing this book, contact this trusted individual and request some counsel, perhaps offer to meet over coffee. During your visit, let them know your past financial experiences; share any areas that you feel you are struggling with. Talk about your new goals and plans on how to reach them (and your reasons WHY). They may notice something that you may have missed. Offer to provide occasional updates (maybe twice a year). This accountability can help you stay on track when you feel like throwing in the towel (taking your money and running).

_____

_____

_____

_____

_____

_____

_____

_____

_____

_____

_____

_____

CHAPTER FIVE

UNDERSTANDING RISKS

MULTIPLY

The sun had not yet risen, and the shipmen were already loading their vessels onto the ship in preparation for their voyage to Lebanon. Abdiel found Benjamin at the docks working to secure several crates.

"Abdiel! How are you, my friend? Did you bring the pomegranates?"

"I would not have forgotten such opportunity, and I thank you again, Benjamin!

The crates are on my cart, would you care to assist?"

"It's the least I can do for a friend, and one-third of the profit of course!" Benjamin said with a wink.

"Of course," Abdiel said, "tell me again, when do you expect to arrive in Lebanon?" Abdiel was holding his cloak firmly below his chin.

"You worry too much my friend! As I said, four days' journey if God smiles upon us."

Abdiel began his journey back home, trying to fight off his uneasiness. *I know Benjamin. He is a just man. All will be well, and besides, by Caleb's counsel, I only traded with a small portion of my master's money with one merchant. I will pray that God will bless my endeavor.*

ENTERING THE WORLD of investing with a healthy, realistic view of risks is vital to a successful investing experience. Many would-be investors recoil at the mention of the word *risk*, believing risk must be a *bad thing*. Images of a casino come to mind, or simply blind speculation, equating risk with a devastating loss. While there are plenty of avenues where an investor can throw caution to the wind, go crazy and "roll the dice," that does not have to be your investing experience.

Searching online for the word *risk*, you'll find such definitions as: (noun) "exposure to the chance of injury or loss;" (verb) "to expose to the chance of loss."

Why take any risk? For the investor, there is an expected reward for the risk taken—the growth of an investment. For a driver, the reward is arriving safely at their intended destination. Both driver and investor have risks they face, and at the same time, there are risks they are able to reduce or avoid.

The driver of a vehicle can reduce their chances of breaking down while on the freeway by assuring proper maintenance of their vehicle; checking fluid levels, tire tread thickness and air pressure, and that all systems are operational (transmission, steering, and brakes). The risk of collision with another vehicle can be reduced (not completely eliminated) by alertness and defensive driving, and never assuming the driver of another vehicle is as alert as you are. A seat and shoulder belt can be worn to reduce injury in the event of a collision, and most cars today have airbags to reduce the *risk* of further injury.

Getting behind the wheel of investing and traveling the roads of the stock markets has its many hazards and risks as well. I will introduce you to the "seat belts and airbags" that can be added to a portfolio for an increased level of safety, as well as make you aware of *the actions of others* that can put you in harm's way.

We will learn which risks can be eliminated, which can be greatly reduced, and those that can be taken on with confidence. Risk can and should be managed.

LIQUIDITY RISK

The inability to access your money without loss of capital or income is known as liquidity risk. Suppose you would like a higher interest rate on the money you have sitting at the bank. A regular savings account might pay an interest rate of .50 of 1%. That is a very low-interest rate, and the reason for this is that the bank understands that you have full access to your money and it's possible that you could withdraw all of that money out at any time because you've made no commitment of time. If you were to purchase a five-year CD (Time Certificate of Deposit), they would offer a higher interest rate because you agree to give the bank use of your money for five years.

Traditionally, you have zero access to your money held in a CD. Any withdrawals before the maturity date of that CD will incur a penalty that can be as much as 12 months' worth of interest. We refer to this as *liquidity risk*.

Let's look at a hypothesis.

John's bank is offering 3% annual interest on a five-year Certificate of Deposit. John decides to place $10,000 into that CD. Three months later, a situation arises in John's life, and he decides he needs his money, and he cashes out his CD. The common early withdrawal penalty on a five-year CD is 12 months of interest, 3% which would be $300. While John earned interest for three months (approximately $75), he will have to pay $300 which is a loss of $225 in principal ($10,075 - $300 = $9,775).

> **Definition:** *maturity date*—the date on which the issuer of the CD stops paying the promised interest rate and the full value of your account is available for withdrawal without paying a fee

Liquidity risk also exists when an investment cannot be easily liquidated into needed cash. Real estate, for example, may be difficult to liquidate when there are no buyers, or when values are low, and you want to avoid selling at a loss. You can prevent liquidity risk in your portfolio through proper diversification in investments that can be sold relatively quickly; stocks, mutual funds, index funds, and bond funds.

INFLATION RISK

The cost of goods and services gradually rise, sometimes year after year. The classic stories from our parents of "When I was a kid" remind us that at some point in history, a candy bar could be had for a nickel! Not so today, the price is closer to a dollar. Obviously, it's not just candy bars that go up in price. We see the price of gasoline fluctuate (usually upwards), property taxes increase, coffee, butter, produce, clothing, and computers, all the good stuff goes up in price. Sometimes, it's flat out demoralizing! This increase in costs is known as *inflation*, and the Government measures it using the Consumer Price Index, or CPI for short. If this CPI increases an average of 3% per year, we could assume that a $30,000 sedan might cost $40,317 in ten years or $54,183.34 in twenty years.

One way to look at it is, it will require more of our dollars to purchase the same items in the future. The buying power of your dollar today will be greatly diminished as time passes. If your savings or investments are earning 2% per year for example, and inflation is at 3%, you are in essence losing 1% per year in purchasing power.

One approach to solving this dilemma is to structure your portfolio with an appropriate portion of equities so that you have a higher expected rate of growth over inflation, helping you maintain or increase the purchasing power of your money in the future. We will address how to plan for this in Chapter 8.

CAPITAL RISK

One of the primary concerns of investors is, "Can I lose my money?" or simply put, "Is my money at risk?" Risk is always a factor when investing in the markets, yet it can be managed and even reduced, according to the specific need of the investor.

Investments fluctuate in value; they move up and they move down. This fluctuation is known as *volatility*. More conservative investments, such as U.S. Treasury Bills, have a lower degree of volatility, and because of the low volatility, the rate of return is also low. Volatility is higher in stocks, especially during short-term periods. While volatility commonly gets a bad rap for being the *threatening* component in the investing experience, it happens to be the very component that provides the potential for growth.

> **Definition:** *volatility*—prices and values tending to
> fluctuate sharply and regularly.

Sure, everybody loves upward volatility (stock prices moving up) and disdains downward volatility (stock prices moving down). This is actually an incorrect thinking due to a lack of knowledge of how the markets work.

Throughout this book, we will look closely at how markets really work so that you can have more confidence in the creation and maintenance of your own investment plan.

"Time heals" may be a myth, but time certainly helps substantially reduce volatility. Stocks historically experience more years of upward movement than years of downward movement and the discipline to stay the course in a prudent investment plan has its rewards—mainly the creation of wealth.

Capital risk can be further reduced by adding Short-Term Fixed Income to your portfolio. This investment category will be explained in chapter 7.

BEHAVIORAL RISK

Sometimes, we are our own worst enemy. We may set out to do well with our finances, with the best of intentions and even seek counsel, but then, our emotions, instincts, and perceptions get in the way, and the wheels fall off!

DALBAR is an independent research firm that, among other things, studies not only market behavior but investor behavior. In 2017, DALBAR concluded a 30-year study of mutual fund sales, redemptions and exchanges each month as the measure of investor behavior. Here's what they found[1]:

Category	1987–2016 Annualized Return
S&P 500	10.16%
DALBAR Individual Investor—Equity Funds	3.98%
CPI (representing inflation)	2.65%

For thirty years of market upturns and downturns, the U.S. Large markets (measured by the index called the S&P 500) still produced an annual average rate of return of 10.16%. During that same period, through the ups and the downs, the average Investor (those tracked by DALBAR) experienced an annual rate of return of only 3.98%.

Why are the returns for the individual investor so low, compared to the broad market? One reason is that investors during the thirty-year study only held their investments for an average of three and a half years. After the three-and-a-half-year mark, they would sell their holdings (selection of investments) and buy all new (to them) investments. Investors

---

1   In its 2017 Quantitative Analysis of Investor Behavior, Dalbar defines "Average Investor" as "The universe of all mutual fund investors whose actions and financial results are restated to represent a single investor. This approach allows the entire universe of mutual fund investors to be used as the statistical sample, ensuring ultimate reliability."

*   The Tech bubble began in the late 1990s and peaked in early 2000, then plummeted, bottoming out by the end of 2001, resulting in a loss in value of approximately $7.1 trillion.

tend to be impatient. In the short-term, if they feel they are not earning as much as they should, or their buddy's investment is doing better, they sell what they have and buy something else.

The study also revealed that investors tend to chase the market, pursuing investment categories that seem to be doing well, at the moment. Sadly, this was not limited to the "Tech Bubble" of the late 1990s when it seemed the whole investing world was screaming that you had to own dot-com companies, or you will miss out on all the wealth.* Bubbles or no bubbles, investors still tend to seek what is "hot" in the investing world, often forsaking a prudent, disciplined investment plan for chasing the wind and hurting themselves in the process.

Active stock-picking is another behavior the study identified as destructive (financially speaking). Stock-picking is the belief that we, or someone else on our behalf, can consistently and predictably pick in advance, which stocks are going to soar in value. Sadly, it is a loser's game. No one can predict the future of individual stocks or the market itself, and we don't believe in crystal balls, do we? Even the "Pros" of Wall Street are unable to consistently and predictably pick winning stocks.

Market-timing is the fourth destructive behavior DALBAR identified that impedes an investor's prospects for growth. This would be any attempt to alter or change the mix of investments in a portfolio based on a prediction or forecast about the future.

So, rather than building a diversified portfolio and holding it long-term, the average investor chases performance, buying a mutual fund or collection of funds based on some ranking system or the advice of a financial consultant.

Emotions are often the culprit of behavioral risk. When values drop, fear kicks in and leads to destructive choices (selling at a loss). When values soar, individual investors can be unrealistically optimistic and crave a higher rate of growth, again, leading to destructive behavior (talking on a higher degree of risk than they should). We will dive into the role that emotions play in our investing experience, in the next chapter.

AVOIDING LIQUIDITY RISK

You can avoid the risk of not having access to your money by faithfully adding to your savings account. What amount do you currently have set aside in the event of a sudden expense?

_____

_____

_____

What amount are you currently adding to your savings on a monthly basis?

_____

_____

_____

_____

If you feel that your current level of saving is inadequate, what reasonable steps can you take to increase the dollar amount of your monthly savings contributions?

_____

_____

_____

_____

_____

AVOIDING INFLATION RISK

With the long-term rate of inflation averaging 4%, the money that you are setting aside for your future income should be positioned to growth at a rate that exceeds the rate of inflation. (Consult a licensed Investment Advisor for an investment plan that is suitable for you). Have you established an account for this goal?

_____

_____

_____

_____

Have you identified the monthly dollar amount that you can commit toward this goal? What is that amount? (This can and should increase over time):

_____

_____

_____

_____

CAPITAL RISK

Proper diversification, and a prudent long-term investment plan, help to reduce Capital risk. You will learn about Diversification in Chapter 7.

BEHAVIORAL RISK

Many investors do the opposite of what they should do during a down market—they sell when they should be buying more—at lower prices.

As you start to build your investing plan, write yourself a note: "Dear future me, when the markets move down and media go crazy with their doom and gloom headlines, breathe, buy more and press on!".

CHAPTER SIX

GUARD YOUR HEART

MULTIPLY

It had been five long days and still no word from Benjamin. Abdiel's mind raced, playing out every possible scenario. Did the ship sink? Had he lost a friend and his investment? Surely, he was not beguiled by this man whom he had known so long. Perhaps the ship had been damaged and the shipmen are still struggling to repair the vessel and bring it to safety?

Abdiel realized that his heart was anxious and that being anxious would not solve the matter. What, or who was he trusting? He purposed in his heart to trust the God of his fathers, the God of Israel.

On the sixth day, Abdiel arrived at the port before the sun rose, hoping to see Benjamin's ship. Around the third hour, he spotted a messenger running toward the port from the North. "Benjamin's ship was caught in a storm," The messenger said, between gasps for air. "There is much damage, but the ship reached land with no loss of life. Most of the cargo was lost or damaged in the storm, only a few crates of metals and tunics survived."

Abdiel was grateful that Benjamin's life was spared, yet he felt crushed by the loss of his investment. He knew there existed such risk. If his master returned today, he would have to report a loss, and that thought grieved him.

"Perhaps I can make up for this loss through other ventures," Abdiel thought, and returned home for further study.

EMOTIONS ARE GREAT AND NECESSARY. As humans, we have an innate desire to be loved; we seek happiness, enjoy pleasurable activities, and also experience sadness and heartache at times. Can you imagine a relationship with someone who exhibits zero emotions? Even the words we speak are often flavored with emotions. Our emotions help us to hold onto precious memories, relate to other people, and make amends with those we've wronged..

While emotions are indeed great and wonderful for relationships, they are absolutely devastating to investing! We are wired to flee pain and pursue pleasures. With the markets moving both up and down, leading investment account balances to soar or plummet, you can imagine the hysterics that ensue as investors react emotionally. "Keep thy heart with all diligence; for out of it are the issues of life" (Proverbs 4:23).

It should come as no surprise that the majority of Scripture that is written on the subject of money and riches are directed toward the heart. It is from the heart that we worry we might not make it financially. It is from the heart that we desire *more.* It is from the heart that we are not satisfied with what we have now.

Unlike the cartoon fairytale, whose moral to the story is *follow your heart,* God's Word warns against trusting the heart because it is "deceitful above all things, and desperately wicked: who can know it?" (Jeremiah 17:9).

We are to guard our heart, with all diligence.

ANXIOUS TO INCREASE WEALTH

Some people have some catching up to do when it comes to accumulating wealth for the future. They may be at a point now when they can start investing a healthy amount on a regular basis, but they don't have the luxury of time that they once had. The tendency is to look for the quickest means to multiply their investing efforts.

Not all *opportunities*, are opportunities at all.

Over 4,800 investors placed their money—in many cases, their life savings—in the investment firm run by a former chairman of National Association of Securities Dealers Automated Quotations exchange (NASDAQ). They were promised consistent returns of 10 percent and 12 percent. Among the 4,800 were: actor Kevin Bacon, a foundation of Steven Spielberg's, and television and radio host, Larry King.

On December 11, 2008, the chairman of this investment firm, Bernard L Madoff, was arrested for running one of the country's largest and longest running Ponzi in history, reporting a loss to investors of nearly $65 Billion.

"They said it is Bernie Madoff, go for it," said Charles Weg of Cherry Hill, New Jersey. It's been eight years since authorities arrested Madoff for bilking billions off investors. Weg's parents were among those left empty-handed, losing their $200,000 investment. It was a financial blow that forced Bea Weg out of her house and into a retirement home where she died in 2012."[1]

---

1   http://6abc.com/finance/local-victims-of-bernie-madoff-this-cant-be-real/1185815/

"So, how did 4,800 investors get drawn into the scheme?" Lita Epstein asks in her March 12, 2009 online article for AOL. com, "Madoff created an aura where people were made to believe they were part of an exclusive club allowed to invest with him. He offered consistently better returns and did so for many years. Then people who were benefiting from these returns told their friends."[2]

Thousands of investors were drawn into a scheme that cost them fortunes, because of a "promise" of very high returns year after year, which would provide faster growth than other traditional investments at that time.

God warns His children of the dangers of desiring to get rich quick. In Proverbs 28:20, we are made aware that, "A faithful man shall abound with blessings: but he that maketh haste to be rich shall not be innocent." And in verse 22, "He that hasteth to be rich hath an evil eye, and considereth not that poverty shall come upon him." Being in a rush to make money will often result in a lack of judgment, such as is the case with Madoff victims. Think about the other common mistakes we make when we are in a hurry. We can drive too fast and get a speeding ticket; injuries are sustained at work when workers are in a hurry or take shortcuts; there's even the contracts or agreements signed in haste without being read.

Breathe, buckle up, and embrace the benefits of staying disciplined over a long period of time.

---

2   https://www.aol.com/2009/03/12/warning-signs-madoff-investors-ignored/

GREED

In 2010, I noticed that one of my clients was making large withdrawals from his IRA that were inconsistent with his usual pattern. Out of concern, I called him to see if everything was all right with him. "Yes, yes everything is fine. I'm going to be putting in a lot more soon!" he replied. A few months passed when I received a call from the fraud department of the company that held his IRA funds. They asked me if I was aware of the withdrawals Bob (not his real name) was making and was there a female calling in these requests? This led me to call Bob again, who now was indignant with me and insisted that everything was great and that soon he will put back more than he took out. I sensed something foul was afoot; I encouraged him to come into my office for a visit to review his finances and long-term plans, but he refused.

Three months later, I received a call from Bob who sounded desperate and asked to come in and see me. Arriving at my office, Bob's demeanor was entirely different. Now, he was in tears, confessing that he had been greedy. When I asked him what happened, he explained that he had received notice that he had won the Canadian Reader's Digest Sweepstakes and was to receive several millions of dollars, but he was "required" to send a cashier's check so that his winnings could "clear customs." They even provided a toll-free number to *Homeland Security* to verify that this process was legitimate and necessary.

After receiving his first $20,000 check, the fraudsters then stated that he needed to pay the taxes in order for his millions to clear. As you may have guessed, he sent more money, in the form of cashier's checks to this phantom company, not the IRS. When it was all said and done, Bob had sent nearly $250,000, from his IRA, which is taxable as income, to these scam artists. Not surprisingly, they stopped taking his calls, and he could no longer reach them. They got what they wanted, and he left with $21,000 to his name and an IRS tax bill of almost $75,000.

PLEASURE AND PAIN

One of the biggest drops in the stock market (since the Great Depression) was during the Credit Crisis of 2008 which resulted in approximately $6.9 trillion in lost value. Picture an emotional 401(k) participant who opens his statement at the end of the year and reads that the U.S. Small Cap funds in his portfolio went down (-38.67%). That hurts! It's emotionally and intellectually painful. Our instincts scream "Run!" and too many do just that—they sell those investments that are down in value and take a loss. This is referred to as a "Realized Loss." He also notices that his Long-Term Government Bonds portion is up +25.8%. This brings pleasure. "I need more of this!" the emotional mind says. Acting on these emotions, this investor then buys the category that is already "up."

Fast forward to the following year. The same investor looks at his statement at the end of 2009 and sees that his recent *favorite* investment, Long-Term Government Bonds, went down (-14.9%) and the category that he bailed out of, U.S. Small Cap, went up +47.54%. He now has suffered three losses; first by knowingly selling at a loss (approx. -39%), second, his new investment went down -14.9%, thirdly the investment he used to own went up +47.54% (representing the lost opportunity for growth). Ouch!

2008 Statement	
Long–Term Gov Bonds +25.80% PLEASURE	**U.S. Small Cap** -38.67% PAIN
Year End 2009 -14.90%	**Year End 2009** +47.54%

These decisions that cause losses are all unnecessary. A prudent investor needs to determine from the onset that he will follow his written investment plan. In such a plan, he will not find a strategy that instructs the investor to panic and sell when values drop, neither chase other investment categories that are temporarily "hot." This is referred to as imprudent investor behavior.

FALSE BRAVADO

We also see another common phenomenon among emotional investors and that is the increased *bravado* or unrealistic optimism they feel as they observe their wealth grow sharply when the markets are *up*. The gains they experience give them an excitement which then leads to comparing their gains with others. They may recognize, for instance, that they have made +12% for the year, but then they see that U.S. Small stocks are up +17%. Now, +12% doesn't seem so exciting anymore; they believe that they should be earning +17%, not +12%. You can probably tell where this is going; this type of investor is driven to buy more U.S. Small Cap (which is already up in value). With the temporary euphoria of "winning," they may even throw caution to the wind and sell the safer holdings in their portfolio (Fixed Income) in order to buy more of that category. That is seemingly *sky-rocketing*. And what are the basic rules for successful investing? Buy when investments are generally low and sell when they are high. Emotion-based decisions lead to breaking these rules and doing just the opposite.

FEAR

"For God hath not given us the spirit of fear; but of power, and of love, and of a sound mind" (2 Timothy 1:7). I submit that fear is the number one source of the destruction of an investment portfolio. Many would adamantly declare that it's the market that can destroy your wealth, and I will show you why they are wrong.

Investors can hurt themselves financially when they make changes to their investments based on their fear. When markets move downward, and portfolio values drop, and the media proclaim that *the end of the world is nigh*, fearful investors often get out of the market, convincing themselves that they will be avoiding any further pain. This causes two financial losses: selling shares at a lower price and experiencing a loss (think about selling your house today for a price reduced by 1/3 of today's value— you most likely, in your right frame of mind, would not sell), and secondly, the loss of growth potential when the markets grow upward, and the investor is "out of the market."

Fear also leads to imprudent behavior such as switching investments because of price changes. Investor A notices that his US Stock portfolio is down 15%, but his friend's, Investor B, investment in Government bonds is up 20%. So, he sells his US Stocks (low price) and Buys Government Bonds (high price). Investor A just broke a simple rule of investing: buy low, sell high. He bought high and sold low, likely losing twice.

TRUSTING RICHES

Our investing experience may go very well, and it is quite possible to amass a respectable sum of money over time. That is something to be thankful for, no doubt. That is also something to be very careful with, as our hearts are easily drawn to wealth and away from God. We may say to ourselves, "I would never turn my back on God," yet wealth has a very strong pull to do just that. In the Book of Hosea, the Bible records that God's chosen people, the Israelites, were so enamored with their wealth and prosperity that "…they were filled, and their heart was exalted; therefore have they forgotten me" (Chapter 13, verse 6). They looked away from God, forgot Him, and worshiped and trusted in their wealth. God judged them for their idolatry by allowing them to be brought into bondage by an enemy nation. Bondage. That is exactly what happens when we allow ourselves to trust in our wealth and not in God. Psalm 62:10 provides guidance for us: "Trust not in oppression, and become not vain in robbery: if riches increase, set not your heart upon them." Also, Paul warned: "Charge them that are rich in this world, that they be not highminded, nor trust in uncertain riches, but in the living God, who giveth us richly all things to enjoy" (1 Timothy 6:17).

Larry Burkett wrote, "It is important to discern the difference between the pride of wealth and the wealth itself. Christ never condemned the wealth—it belongs to God. He condemned the wealthy-minded of this world."[3]

---

3   Using Your Money Wisely, Larry Burkett. 1985 Christian Financial Concepts; page 27

*   US Small Stocks represented by CRSP 6-10 index. Source: DFA Returns Software. Past Performance is guarantee of future results

✍ PUTTING IT INTO PRACTICE

Can you identify the cultural messages, and personal mindset about money that fight against your investing peace of mind? List some here:

_____

_____

_____

_____

_____

_____

_____

_____

Which Bible principle(s) will you apply to your life, to help guard your heart?

_____

_____

_____

_____

_____

_____

_____

What verse(s) will you meditate on?

_____

_____

_____

_____

_____

_____

CHAPTER SEVEN

THE BENEFITS OF DIVERSIFICATION

MULTIPLY

While searching the writings of Solomon, Abdiel noticed that the infamous king taught the wisdom of casting your bread upon the waters, for thou shalt find it after many days. "That's it! What was I thinking, placing such wealth on only one ship, and suffering loss? If I spread my master's wealth upon many waters, giving a portion to seven or eight ships, I will increase the potential for gain and reduce the risk of loss. How likely will seven ships suffer the storms?"

He dedicated the next seven days to learning the various trade routes and meeting the merchantmen who sailed these routes.

KING SOLOMON is known for being the wisest person who ever lived. The fame of his wisdom spread across the known world (Think about how slow information would have traveled without the Internet!). Even the Queen of Sheba journeyed all the way to Jerusalem from Ethiopia, in an attempt to disprove the rumors she had heard.

In 1 Kings 9 and 10, we read that King Solomon actually had a navy of ships and "shipmen that knew the sea." Now, what comes to your mind when you read, "a navy of ships?" For me, I start hearing "Anchors away!" in my head, along with images of battleships. Go Navy!

But wait, why would Solomon have a navy of ships? Do we know of any wars that Solomon fought? No. He was a king of peace. So, why would this peaceable king have a navy of ships? A little closer inspection will reveal that these were *merchant* ships and that Solomon traded goods with Ophir and Tarshish, "bringing gold, and silver, ivory, and apes, and peacocks" (1 Kings 10:22b). Because of Solomon's wisdom and fame, people from all over gave valuable gifts to Solomon, and he sent his servants and shipmen to fetch these gifts from many faraway lands. What does this have to do with investing, you may be wondering?

This background helps us understand the practical application of Ecclesiastes 11:1–2: "Cast thy bread upon the waters: for thou shalt find it after many days. Give a portion to seven, and also to eight; for thou knowest not what evil shall be upon the earth."

If Solomon were to have all of his goods and treasures on one single ship, he understood that the risk would be great, and there would be a high probability that this one ship would be damaged by storm, crashed upon rocks, or overtaken by thieves.

However, if he divided his goods among seven or eight ships, he would spread out his wealth and lower his risk of loss. One ship may suffer loss, but the other six or seven would be expected to return safely.

There are many benefits to properly diversifying your investment portfolio. (We use the word *portfolio* to describe the range of investments held in one or more accounts).

REDUCTION OF RISK

It is common for someone to own shares of stock of the company they work for. They believe they know the company well enough and are confident in its financial and business strength. Many companies offer their employees a plan through which they can conveniently buy company stock at a discount through a payroll deduction. This is called an ESOP (Employee Stock Ownership Plan). The time for caution is when that company's stock is the only investment in their portfolio or the majority of one's investments. They do not have diversification working for them. All of their *eggs* are in one basket, so to speak. They have greatly increased the potential for loss.

No matter how great a company you may work for is, there are far too many factors that can cause its stock price to fluctuate drastically: a competitor gets sued, and your company is "guilty by association;" new regulations may limit, restrict or outlaw the nature of your company's business, or the industry simply loses favor (the coal industry, for instance, took a big hit in the final years of the Obama Administration).

In addition, 2008 taught us that no company is "too big to fail." Do you remember Chrysler, Washington Mutual, Citigroup, Lehman Bros, GM, Worldcom, Enron, and PG&E? These are all huge corporations which, despite their mammoth sizes, all filed for bankruptcy, resulting in a loss of over $1 Billion (in the top ten bankruptcies).[1]

When you own stock in only one company, and the price of that stock drops or disappears altogether, your wealth is devastated.

But when you own stock in many companies, across many categories that are not closely related to each other, you have the potential of achieving higher returns (growth) with lower risk. This is referred to as low correlation, and it is the key to diversification.

> **Definition:** *correlation*—the relationship between
> two investments

What we are looking for are investment categories with price movements that are not similar to each other, so that when one goes down, the other has good potential of offsetting it by increasing or remaining level. Think of the "teeter-totter"

---

1   http://instantshift.com/2010/02/03/22-largest-bankruptcies-in-world-history/

that used to be in playgrounds. One side goes down, and the other side goes up.

As an example, if local labor laws in Brazil hinder the production of coconut water, which results in a drop in this small company's stock price, it is not likely to impact the stock prices of large companies in the United States—it is a localized issue impacting a few international small companies. This could represent one risk, or an "…evil" that "…shall be upon the earth." Proper diversification can help protect you from that "evil."

To further illustrate, if half of a portfolio consists of small international companies (A), and the other half is large U.S. companies (B), it is likely that when one category is down, the other may be up or not move at all. See illustration below:

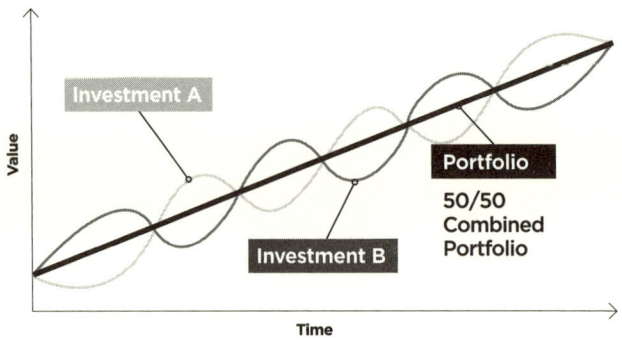

Notice the line in the center. Hypothetically, it represents balance—a steadying of fluctuations, resulting in less volatility while maintaining the potential for growth. When we own many investment categories that are not closely related, we spread our risk across different waters. One or more investment categories may decrease in value while the others are likely to increase or maintain. "…for thou knowest not what evil shall be upon the earth" (Ecclesiastes 11:2b).

We cannot know what the markets will do tomorrow or next year. But we can diversify to eliminate having too much of our "bread" on just one "ship." An investor who had all or most of their investments in the S&P 500 in 2008 would have experienced a monumental loss in value during the *housing, or, credit crisis.*

However, those who were properly diversified, having only a small portion of their investments in the S&P 500 and the remaining portions in other investment categories (the other 6 or 7 ships) would most likely avoid a drop-in value to the extent the S&P 500 suffered (-54% within five months).

MAXIMIZE GROWTH POTENTIAL

It is very encouraging to learn that Solomon spread his wealth and investments across many waters, and we have that same opportunity today to invest in companies across the seas— this is referred to as International investing.

There are many countries, in addition to the U.S. (about forty-four of them), that have free markets and publicly traded companies which produce goods or services. A country is said to have a Free Market when there is: Rule of Law, Property Rights, and Patent protection.

Some of these International companies are in investment categories (we call them *Asset Classes*) which have higher long-term expected rates of return than the large U.S. companies category.

Small international company stocks, as a class, have grown by an annual rate of 14.24% (from 1970 to 2016), whereas large U.S. companies (as measured by the S&P 500) have averaged 10.02% per year (from 1927 to 2016).[2] This does not mean that we should put all the money we have into the category with the highest rate of return. With this higher expected growth rate comes increased volatility. For this reason, it is not a good idea to invest heavily in just one of these asset categories but rather to own small portions of many, different asset categories.

"Own a lot of asset categories to benefit from their different growth expectations over time."

HOW TO DIVERSIFY?

Let's take a closer look at the *ingredients* that can make up a diversified portfolio (as identified by Academics in the field). The following list represents a handful of the varying categories that stocks commonly fall into and their historic average rate of growth. It is helpful to get to know these category names so that you can identify them when selecting Funds for your investment portfolio. "Give a portion to seven, and also to eight; for thou knowest not what evil shall be upon the earth…" (Ecclesiaste 11:2).

Market capitalization "Cap," represents the total dollar market value of a company's outstanding shares. A

---

2   The various market segments represent Index data derived from DFA Returns software 12/15

Annualized Capital Return		
U.S. Large Stocks	10.02%	1926-2017
U.S. Large Value Stocks	12.03%	1926-2017
U.S. Small Cap Value	14.91%	1926-2017
U.S. Micro Cap	12.38%	1926-2017
International Large	9.28%	1970-2017
International Small Cap	14.24%	1970-2017
Fixed income	4.74%	1972-2017

company that issued 250 million shares, and the share price (stock price) is $50 per share, would have a market capitalization of $12.5 billion.

"Value stocks" are companies that have a lower market price than other companies relative to their size. These types of companies are usually experiencing some kind of financial distress, and usually, their earnings are down. As a result, they are riskier and offer investors the potential for a higher return.

It may seem counter-intuitive to own such companies based on this description, but companies have an incentive to not only survive but thrive, and when we own a portion of this category, we expect a *reward* for taking on the additional risk— over time. Some Index and Mutual funds in this category will hold hundreds of companies which also helps spread the risk.

HOW TO OWN THESE ASSET CATEGORIES

It is fascinating to learn that Solomon spread his wealth and investments across seven and even eight different *investments* (possibly exports on several ships), and we have that same opportunity today to invest in companies across the seas—with International funds.

It would be costly and inefficient to try and purchase individual stocks in each of these investment categories. If you were able to pay as little as $7 transaction fee to buy shares in one company, and you want to own 100 companies, that would be $700 in fees!

Today, we have access to vehicles which hold hundreds—even thousands—of companies packaged in one investment called a Fund. There are Mutual Funds, Index Funds, and Exchange-Traded Funds (ETF's) which afford us the ease of owning shares of thousands of companies by purchasing only a few funds.

MUTUAL FUNDS

With the objective of making it affordable to invest in a wide selection of securities, mutual funds made their public appearance in 1928 and really grew in popularity in the 1980s and 1990s. Today, a mutual fund manager builds a portfolio of stocks (or Bonds) with as many as 90 to 200 or more companies to be held in his "Fund." Investors buy shares of this mutual fund which then gives them partial ownership in as many companies.

These mutual funds, as financial products, have names which generally attempt to describe which category they seek to represent. "ACME Large Cap Fund," "XYZ

International Small," or even "ABC Total Market Fund" are hypotheticals. Yet, there are many mutual funds with obscure names which may not clearly describe which of these asset categories it owns. Names such as "Conservative Wealth Strategy," "Relative Value Fund," "Dynamic Allocation Fund," and "Infrastructure Fund" really do not provide us with details by title. To add to that complexity, there are approximately 28,000 mutual funds out there to choose from. We will take a closer look at practical approaches to choosing funds for your portfolio in the next chapter.

Retail mutual funds have managers who choose which stocks will make up the fund, and according to Morningstar, they tend to actively trade, turning over their stocks to the tune of 60%-90% per year—which means for every one hundred companies owned by the fund, the manager is dumping 60-90 of them and replacing them with 60-90 new companies. This is known as active trading and may not result in the highest rates of return for you.

INDEX FUNDS

An Index is the lower-priced cousin to the mutual fund. We can view Index funds as a type of mutual fund that has been designed to closely match or track the components of a market index like the Russell 2000 (Small companies) and the *darling* of Wall Street (sarcasm intended), the S&P 500. Unlike mutual funds which are typically *active*, index funds tend to be more *passive*, more of a *buy and hold* approach to investing.

Index funds typically have lower expenses because they are not as active in placing trades and they do not have to pay for as much research as mutual funds because they are simply trying to mimic the performance of an index. As the S&P 500 tracks the top 500 US Large companies, S&P 500 *index* funds will look to own a cross-section of those same 500 companies. There is no guesswork, just own what the S&P owns, which seldom changes. When we keep expenses down in our portfolios, we are able to keep more of the growth gained in our investments.

EXCHANGE-TRADED FUNDS (ETFS)

ETFs are like the Index Fund's cooler younger brother. They are alike in that they track a particular index, are passive, and have lower fund expenses. They are different in that an ETF trades like a stock, meaning that they can be purchased or sold in real-time during *market hours*, and you can observe price changes throughout the trading day. This can work against the investor who wishes to stay disciplined over time. Just because we *can* get in and out of an ETF quickly, does not mean we *should*. (We will look at Investor Behavior in chapter nine).

Mutual funds and index funds *settle* at the end of the trading day. That means we are unable to know the price or value of our fund until that evening, or the next trading day. It also means that if we wanted to liquidate some of our mutual fund holdings at 9:15 AM, we would not know the value of that transaction until 4:30 PM EST as that is the time the markets close in New York.

ETFs can go a little farther into the obscure than Index Funds. There are ETFs that niche down into specific industries where Index Funds do not. There are HealthCare Industry ETFs and even Automotive ETFs.

In this chapter, we have learned the benefits of diversification, were introduced to many investment categories (asset classes) with low correlation to each other, and looked at a few *vehicles* which allow us to own thousands of companies at a fraction of the cost of buying them all individually. In the next chapter, we will look at practical methods by putting it all together in a portfolio which can be designed to weather the inevitable in *good and bad times* of the economy, the political climate, geopolitical tensions, wars, and whatever the media can throw at us!

Would you be able to explain the benefits of diversification to a 14-year-old?

_____

_____

_____

_____

_____

_____

How would you explain these benefits in your own words?

_____

_____

_____

_____

_____

_____

Do you currently have diversification working in your favor, or do you need to make some adjustments?

_____

_____

_____

_____

What steps, if applicable, will you take in order to benefit from diversification?

_____

_____

_____

_____

CHAPTER EIGHT

BUILDING YOUR PORTFOLIO

MULTIPLY

"A half shekel for every two shekels paid every summer. That is my rate," announced the exchanger quite proudly. The man was combing his beard with the fingers of one hand and eating bread dipped in oil with another.

"I would ask for one shekel for every two shekels I place with you," replied Abdiel, in the most confident tone he could muster at the moment.

"One shekel! No one pays such usury!" snorted the exchanger, pieces of bread now leaping out of his mouth.

"I, uh, I believed that was the going rate in Jerusalem," Abdiel said.

The exchanger only glared silently, his chest heaving up and down as he breathed loudly.

Abdiel thought quickly. He could see that the exchangers were not as willing to barter as the silk traders and farmers were. He finally consented.

"Yes, of course. That is acceptable. One-half shekel repaid for every two shekels I place with you. I wish to place forty shekels with you, and I will return in one year's time."

The man made a great show of his inscribing a receipt for Abdiel, huffing, puffing, and swallowing loudly.

Abdiel thought it wise to retain a portion with the exchangers—money that would be available for his use if he needed it, as much of the wealth will be traded in various forms of goods; vessels of silver, linens, silks, spices, and fruit.

KEEPING MONEY in the bank is boring, and pays very little interest, but it serves a valuable purpose in our financial picture. When an expense or a need for a purchase arises, we should draw money from our bank account, not from our investment account. Money in the bank is not exposed to the volatility of the stock market, while investments in the stock market fluctuate in value daily. We are expecting higher rates of return on our long-term investments, not our savings.

BAKING A CAKE, AND BUILDING A PORTFOLIO

A recipe for building a portfolio is similar to a recipe for baking a chocolate cake. I love moist, rich, chocolate cake. But in order to enjoy the desired moist chocolate cake, I'm going to need the proper ingredients, and in the proper proportion.

Now, if I have a personal bias and really love butter (just for example), excessive butter is not going to help me reach my goal. Buying three different brand names of butter and tripling the proportion of my favorite ingredient is not going to help me. The result is going to be a very unsavory goop, not a moist, fluffy chocolate cake. My wife is a skilled baker (I'm a lucky man), and she will need the proper balance of the required ingredients because if she has too much of one thing, we will not be able to enjoy the delicious treat we desire. On the other hand, if she does not add *enough* butter, it will be a disaster as well.

Once we have all the ingredients and have put them all together in proper proportion, we can now put the plan into place. This is going to take some time. If she pulls the cake out of the oven too early, we're not going to have cake. She will have wasted all of the ingredients. If she lets it bake too long, the cake will be destroyed. It needs to bake for the prescribed amount of time. When we've reached that time, the cake needs to be taken out of the oven *carefully*, so that it doesn't fall.

The same method applies to your investment plan. While there are many *ingredients*, we do not want to be too heavy in only one asset class, even if it is our *favorite*.

ADDING A DEGREE OF "CUSHION" TO YOUR PORTFOLIO

Within an investment portfolio, there is a place for this "boring" money also. I introduced fixed income in the previous chapter, and it plays an increasingly important role as we get older and closer to retirement.

We expect equities to provide a greater degree of growth for us over time. The more time we have before the need to withdraw our money, the greater portion of our portfolio we can allocate to equities. As we approach the time horizon in which we will need to access our invested dollars, we should gradually increase the portion of fixed income in our portfolio to provide a higher level of *cushion* against volatility.

Fixed income usually consists of short-term bonds, intermediate bonds, and cash. Bonds are known for their safety, in that when held to their maturity date, they *mature*, and you receive the return of your principle, plus you've earned a little bit of interest.

As the values of these bonds do not fluctuate to the degree that equities fluctuate (especially when you have short-term bond funds), they can serve as a cushion to your portfolio, should the markets take a downturn. The portion of your portfolio invested in equities may decrease in value, while your fixed income portion remains steadier. (Bonds are issued to pay a set rate of interest during its maturity period (which can vary from a couple of years up to thirty years). If interest rates rise and new bonds are issued which pay a higher interest rate than previously issued bonds, investors are more likely to purchase the new bonds, and not the old bonds. Would you rather buy a \$5,000 bond that pays 3.0% per year or 2.3% per year? To sell the older bond (paying 2.3% in this example), the bond would have to be sold at a discount to make up for the difference in interest—resulting in a partial loss of principle. Short-term bonds can help eliminate this type of loss because they mature quicker, so there is less exposure to interest rate risk.)

We've looked at diversification and understand that a prudent portfolio should hold asset categories that are not closely related to each other.

What will your investment portfolio look like? That will depend greatly on your age and your ability and willingness to endure seasons when your investment values are down. If you have the healthy, long-term view that growth comes from owning the markets and you have twenty years or more before you may need income, then a portfolio that is heavily weighted in equities, diversified across many asset categories, may serve you well.

You may be reading this book and thinking that you have five years or less before you may need to draw income out of your investments. Would investing in equities still be prudent? I would submit that yes, it is prudent, but with a smaller portion allocated to equities and more of your portfolio allocated to fixed income.

Many investors make the mistake of avoiding equity exposure, which is where growth comes from. During your retirement years, you will still be affected by the rising cost of living. Consequently, it is important to continue having a degree of growth on your money so that you can keep ahead of the eroding effects of inflation.

The rate of inflation, at the date of this writing, is relatively low. I believe it is wise to plan for higher rates of inflation in the future and to structure your investments to stay above that rate as inflation erodes the buying power of your dollars.

To illustrate, if someone were to place all of their investment dollars in the bank at retirement, earning .50% interest and inflation is 3%, they are effectively losing 2.5% per year in the buying power of their money and take the risk of running out of money during their lifetime.

Whereas, if their portfolio were to be structured conservatively yet with just enough allocated to equities so as to experience 4% or 5% average annual growth over time, their wealth could stay ahead of inflation and allow them a better opportunity for their money to last throughout their lifetime.

THE IMPORTANT RELATIONSHIP BETWEEN RISK AND RETURN

As much as we may dream of getting stock market rates of growth while having the risk level of a savings account—that's not going to happen! Because more risk is involved, stocks have the potential to provide a higher rate of return than fixed income instruments. Over long periods of time, the market has historically rewarded equity investing. This does not necessarily mean that you are going to try and "knock it out of the park!", and with reckless abandon, buy the highest risk funds available. But it should mean that you can, with the help of your Investment Advisor, structure a globally and domestically diversified portfolio to suit your need for growth, in line with your personal tolerance for the ups and downs of the markets.

AN AGGRESSIVE ALLOCATION

For those who seek a higher average rate of return and are willing to soldier through times of volatility, an aggressive portfolio may be suitable. This portfolio mix would generally contain up to 95% US and International Equities, and 5% Fixed Income. That 95% in equities can be allocated among the asset classes we looked at earlier in order to benefit from diversification; a portion to US Large, US Large Value, US Small, US Small Value, International Large, International Small (See your Investment professional for specific recommendations).

An investor who sets up an aggressive portfolio for the purpose of seeking a higher annual rate of return, over a long period of time, accepts that there will be periods in which the value of their investments may be down to 10, 20, maybe even 30 percent. Stated as simple numbers, they don't *sound* so threatening, but seeing actual dollars in the negative can stir some emotions. When a statement arrives, and you see a previous balance of $200,000 has become $140,000, you could feel some fear. Keep calm and press on, this is not a *real* (realized) loss unless the emotional decision to *sell it all* is made (not at all recommended). This is actually a great opportunity to buy more, while your quality investments are on sale at lower prices. Markets historically recover, and often faster than we think. After a huge downturn in the markets in 2008, the US markets (as measured by the CRSP 1-10) went on to triple in value from 1/2009 through December 2016.[1] So, hypothetically, this portfolio that dropped from $200,000 down to $140,000 could have grown to $420,000 by December 2016.

ALLOCATING FOR GROWTH, WITH A SHORTER TIME HORIZON

When there is a need for growth but not as long of a time horizon before the funds are needed for income, say, in eight to ten years, then the equities portion could be dialed down to 75%-85%, and the fixed income, which cushions the volatility,

---

1   Index information derived from DFA Returns Software 12/16 citing the CRSP 1-10. This example is for illustrative purposes only. Indices are unmanaged, cannot be invested in directly and do not include management fees, transaction costs or expenses. No representation is made that your investments will achieve similar results.

*   Past performance is no guarantee of future success. Consult an investment professional for personalized recommendations.

would represent the other 15%-25% of your portfolio balance. The goal of structuring your portfolio with these sample allocations would be to seek a reasonably high rate of return, long-term, without the full degree of capital risk of being "all-in" the stock market.

Increasing the portion of fixed income in this portfolio structure will increase the *cushion*, resulting in lower volatility, and also a little less expected growth. When you hear that the "markets are up 12% for the year," hypothetically, do not expect your portfolio to experience that same growth, because 15%–25% of your money is not in the stock market. This is part of the plan. Conversely, when you hear that the "markets are down 12%," you would not expect your portfolio to drop by the same degree. Why? Because this portfolio structure has reduced its exposure to the market, having a portion in fixed income (which we do not expect to be as volatile as stocks).

A MODERATE ALLOCATION

What if there are only five years before the retirement goal? A portfolio consisting of 50% fixed income and 50% equities could serve us well, provided we stay emotionally disciplined through turbulent times in the market. One of the primary goals of structuring a portfolio in this manner is the preservation of capital, over time, while seeking growth that would stay ahead of the rate of inflation.

Keep in mind that when the markets go down, only 50% of the portfolio is exposed to equities in this scenario, and that 50% is spread across potentially thousands of companies in dozens of countries—allowing the benefit of diversification to help reduce (not eliminate) the downward movement and maximize growth for the level of risk we've decided to take.

During the market crash of 2008, the S&P 500 (which is one category—US Large Cap) was one of the biggest losers, dropping an estimated -54% from October 2008 through February 2009, but long-term US Government Bonds shot up in the double digits!

In this hypothetical 50/50 portfolio (50% in fixed income and 50% Diversified Equities), 50% of your money is sheltered from the equities market, and only a fraction of your portfolio (depending on how you allocated) is invested in the S&P 500, greatly reducing your risk of loss of value.

A CONSERVATIVE ALLOCATION

When the primary concern is to preserve the value of your investment account but still seeking growth to help keep up with inflation, we would want a portfolio that is highly weighted in the fixed income category for stability, with a portion still invested in equities, properly diversified globally and domestically. An allocation of 60% fixed income and 40% equities helps accomplish that goal. It will not eliminate, but greatly reduce the volatility in your portfolio and allow the opportunity for growth over time.

Check with your licensed professional for guidance as to the portfolio allocation that is best for you.

THE MARKET IS DOWN, DID I LOSE?

It is not the markets that devastate portfolios; it is investors' behavior.

I stopped keeping track of the value of my home. Why? Because I am still living in it and have no intention, in the short-term, of selling it—so, the current or even monthly change in value has no significance for me. Our money feels like it is another matter, but it isn't if you set out to benefit from long-term investing. The markets move every day, and it is not necessary nor wise to look at your balance so frequently.

The Stock Market's sometimes move down, that's part of its nature. Down markets actually provide buying opportunities for disciplined investors. When good investments go down in price, that's a great time to buy more! In fact, those enrolled in 401(k)s or other Employer-Sponsored plans, do so automatically as they contribute (purchase funds) each pay period; they are buying shares "on sale" because of the lower prices.

What if you are no longer adding to your investments, and you see the balance of your sizable portfolio go down by, say, $10,000. Did you lose $10,000? No. A loss occurs when you make the conscious decision (often irrational and emotional) to sell when the values are down. When you stay disciplined through the downturns, you will see decreased values, but these are not losses. Historically, market downturns are temporary, and market recovery (upturns) happens quickly, often sooner than expected.

🖺 PUTTING IT INTO PRACTICE

Have you identified the time period in which you might start withdrawing money out of your investment account(s) (perhaps a retirement date)?

_____

_____

_____

_____

_____

How many years do you have prior to that date?

_____

_____

_____

_____

Do you believe your investment account is (or, will be) structured appropriately for your time horizon?

_____

_____

_____

_____

Remember, growth is expected from the stocks, mutual funds, and index funds in a portfolio over time, and with these is volatility, the likelihood that values can rise or drop steeply. A general rule is to start increasing the fixed income portion of your portfolio as you near the time you expect to start taking withdrawals, providing a cushion from the volatility of the markets. As of now, what percentage of your account is in equities (stocks, mutual funds, index funds?)

_____

_____

_____

_____

_____

As of now, what percentage of your account is in fixed income?

_____

_____

_____

_____

_____

CHAPTER NINE

SPECULATING AND GAMBLING VS. PRUDENT INVESTING

"Behold, Abdiel, I have placed before you this opportunity," said Michael, the old man who owned land south of Abdiel's lord. "Delay not in your answer, for I have found favor in the eyes of the Parthians and they desire greatly to purchase my silks. I own the silk trade from Xiongnu, but this enterprise is too much for one man, and the travel is costly and laborious. Buy from me my silk. I will offer you a reduced price, and you then can sell to the Parthians for great gain."

Michael's proposal seemed very lucrative. He showed Abdiel the trade route from Asia Minor across the Mediterranean Sea, then by land to Parthia. Many laborers, camels, and provision were needed for each expedition, but the opportunity for profit was great. Abdiel's investment would help expand the silk trade and allow for additional expeditions, thus an increase in silk and trade.

NOT EVERY INVESTMENT *opportunity* is a sound investment. By the late 1990s, the internet had taken the world by storm. This "Information Superhighway" stepped into our lives and not only grabbed our attention but grabbed a lot of investment dollars as well. The media spread stories of young nobodies becoming dot-com millionaires overnight. Business magazines were touting companies like CMGI as "A screaming buy," and WorldCom's stock price as being "Dirt cheap," and of Global Crossing, "Could triple in a year!"* In the money world, all eyes were on website and tech companies, and the clarion call was "Get in or get left behind!"

Trillions of investor dollars poured into the stocks of these new technology and dot-com "companies," only to find out soon after the *frenzy* that many of these companies were not companies at all, in that they had no assets, non-revenue streams on the books and that sector, as measured by the NASDAQ, took a sharp and deadly dive. An estimated 7.1 trillion dollars, representing the hopes and dreams of people like you and me, were wiped out in a matter of months.[1]

Real people, with real hopes and dreams, lost their very real fortunes in pursuit of an *opportunity* that was not a prudent investment after all, only a hot *trend* that turned out to be one of the largest market *bubbles** in recent history.

The tech bubble of 1999-2002 proved to be a costly lesson in speculating and chasing *hot sectors*.

---

[1]   Dr. Jean-Paul Rodrigue, Dept. Of Global Studies & Geography, Hofstra University

*   Fortune Magazine, July 24, 2000

> **Definition:** *speculate*—to engage in any business transaction involving considerable risk or the chance of large gains, especially to buy and sell commodities, stocks, etc., in the expectation of a quick or very large profit (Dictionary.com)

It may sometimes be difficult to distinguish between speculation and investment, and whether an activity qualifies as speculative or investing can depend on some factors, including the nature of the asset, the expected duration of the holding period, and the amount of leverage.[2]

"For better or for worse, the gambling instinct is part of human nature—so it's futile for most people even to try suppressing it. But must confine and restrain it. That's the single best way to make sure you will never fool yourself into confusing speculation with investment." —Jason Zweig, commentary in Benjamin Graham's *The Intelligent Investor.*[3]

GOLD

You may have seen the infomercials—the ones with a grey-haired Hollywood actor who hasn't acted in Hollywood in years, warning us of the National Debt, the devaluation of the U.S. Dollar, inflation, and the coming economic collapse. The solution? Gold of course!

The companies selling gold used such phrases, as spoken by the actor, "Do your part and protect your future, buy gold."[4]

---

2   http://www.investopedia.com/terms/s/speculation.asp Accessed 12/08/2018

3   The Intelligent Investor—Revised Edition, by Benjamin, Graham, Harper Collins, 1973, New material: 2003 by Jason Zweig.

4   Commercial promoting Gold: https://www.youtube.com/watch?v=S1HrVdLmkhk

Their underlying message is, when the economy dives, you'll have gold and be safe. This plays upon our fears and points us back to the days when the U.S. dollar was backed by gold, giving us a false sense that we could pay our bills and stay ahead of an economic crash by physically owning gold. Is this true?

Franklin Delano Roosevelt took our country off the gold standard in 1933. Great Britain dropped it in 1931, Australia in 1929, as well as Japan. If so many world powers ditched gold as a back-up to their country's currency, why is there such a push to buy gold?

Let's begin with a quick review of a basic investing "rule:" Buy Low, Sell High. Pretty basic. When you have many investment companies that have been buying gold over the past decade or two at $200-$300 an ounce, they are motivated to sell their gold at higher prices, gladly spending hundreds of thousands of dollars in advertising, artificially boosting the demand for gold. When demand is high, prices increase. If they can sell you gold at $1,200 an ounce, that they purchased at $200-$300 an ounce (hypothetically), wouldn't that be lucrative?

Buying gold is speculating, believing that the value of your gold purchase will increase in value and that you will make a lot of money. Gold is a metal, not a publicly traded company. It has no employees, no earnings to report, no taxes to pay. How then would anyone expect it to increase in value? Because it is scarce? There are several gold mines on this planet which continue to mine gold out of this sphere (earth) and can continue to do so beyond our life expectancies. So, it cannot be the rarity factor.

OTHERS WANT YOUR MONEY

During the height of the recent "Gold Rush," when the price per ounce was dancing around the $1,750 range, gold companies were all over the major media pitching gold as a hedge against "the falling dollar." Had an investor purchased gold at that time, they would have seen a very brief increase in price followed by a devastating drop. To illustrate, an investment of $100,000 in August 2011, the time when the owner of a leading gold investment corporation declared, "There is no ceiling to the price gold" would have lost -$32,046 in value by December 2015. Apparently, there is no *floor*, either.

REAL ESTATE INVESTMENT TRUSTS (REITS)

Some investors would like to invest in real estate, believing that there is a limited supply of *dirt* on this planet. Thus, the law of supply and demand should cause values to increase steadily. The housing bubble of 2007-2009 should have taught us otherwise. During this time, the value of U.S. households fell by nearly $6 trillion. As late as October 2012, 65 percent of all U.S. housing markets still had average prices lower than before the 2008 financial crisis.[5] At least, 792,000 homeowners in America actually lost their house through foreclosure in

---

5   https://www.washingtonpost.com/business/economy/housing-picture-65-percent-of-markets-worse off than-before-the-bust/2012/10/22/2b824ecc-1c73-11e2-ba31-3083ca97c314_story.html?utm_term=.be3239a3c85b

2012, and as of this writing bank foreclosures are still running at a rate of over 40,000 a month. In January 2014, there were 822,000 foreclosures in America and in January 2015, there were 549,000 homes in some form of foreclosure.[6]

Diversification and income are what attracts most investors to REITs. A REIT may hold numerous properties including apartment complexes, office buildings, and hospitals. It may even invest in mortgages, giving the investor a sense of safety through diversification.

The problem is, while there may be multiple real estate holdings within that investment vehicle, you, the investor, still only own category—real estate, which is not an academically identified asset class in terms of owning equities. In fact, the returns (rate of growth) of REITs is inferior to equities.

Another concern with REITs is the matter of liquidity, or in this case, illiquidity. Some REITs sold by stockbrokers are not publicly traded, and because of that, you cannot simply go online and sell some or all of your holdings in that investment. Often, liquidity (availability to your money) is limited to once every three months, and even then, only a portion of your balance is available for distribution.

As with any potential investment, *caveat emptor—let the buyer beware.*

---

6   http://www.corelogic.com/research/foreclosure-report/national-fore-closure-report-january-2015.pdf

STOCK PICKING

Some investors believe that they can have relative safety and growth through investing in good old solid companies that seem to have been around forever. Stock in these companies, often referred to as "Blue Chip" stocks, seem to be *too big to fail*. Recent history proves otherwise. Do you remember Washington Mutual? How about WorldCom? Circuit City or even Lehman Brothers? Gone. These are just a handful of many former behemoths that disappeared along with the wealth that was once created by their stock values. Other big names have filed for bankruptcy (or came close, like Citigroup) or received government bailouts as did General Motors.

Which company's stocks should someone have in their portfolio? Should an investor own the big companies, those that are too big to fail? Should an investor seek out the newest technology and take a chance with a promising upstart company? Should you use sophisticated software with its indicators as to which stocks are positioned to soar?

That kind of sounds like gambling to me. The academic evidence is clear, and overwhelmingly against stock-picking as a reliable, consistent, predictable method for long-term investing success.

Stock picking, as an investment approach, is based on the hope that someone can pick the stocks that will do well in the future, beat other stocks, or beat the market in general. Not only do they have the arduous task of picking the right stocks right now, but must also continue to do so consistently, predictably, and all through their accumulation years. Is this even possible? Is it practical? To help answer those questions, let's look to the pros who regularly pick stocks on a much larger scale than you or I might.

Mutual fund managers buy and sell shares of company stocks by the hundreds of thousands. According to Morningstar, the average retail mutual fund has a turnover of 60%-80%. That means if a mutual fund owns shares of 100 different companies, that fund manager will sell 60-80 of those companies and replace them with another 60-80 companies— within twelve months. That sounds like stock-picking to me! Are they successful at it? Not according to the data.

Using data from CRSP (Center for Research and Stock Pricing, University of Chicago School of Business*), an investment of $10,000 in the average of all U.S. equity mutual funds (managed by fund managers) would have grown, from 1972 through 2016, to $387,550.57. This data includes the performance of mutual funds that were closed down because of great losses. Before you get too impressed, that same $10,000 in the S&P 500 (which has no manager), during the same period would have grown to approximately $699,963.92

The U.S. markets, which are not managed, but organic, being driven by the laws of supply and demand—provided almost twice the potential growth of those funds that were managed (and seemingly actively-traded) by fund managers. If the big guys can't seem to pick the right stocks consistently, would you really want to attempt to pick the right stocks, consistently and persistently throughout your working years?

TRACK RECORD INVESTING

An investor shuffles through the stack of glossy pages of investment choices they just received for setting up their new investment account, and they go straight to the performance page. Their eyes follow their finger as it scrolls down the column displaying, "Average Annual Return," looking for the largest number. "Well, this mutual fund has knocked it out of the park for the past ten years, so it must be good!" This is a common assumption in the mutual fund selection process. Many investors choose this method because they can *view* larger rates of return in shorter periods (one-year average, five-year, and ten-year averages, for example) right there on a printed report—so they believe it must be true.

Here's what is often promoted in the annals of Wall Street marketing; finding funds that did well in the past is a reliable indicator of which funds will do well in the future. But, does this work? Is this a dependable method for choosing your investments? Remember, money, and everything that money brings in life is at stake here.

Let's go back to the data from CRSP. Looking at the top 30 U.S. mutual funds' returns from 2007 to 2011, we would see an average annual rate return of +5.07%. Not bad at all, considering the terrible market downturn of 2008 and 2009, and during that same period, the average of all U.S. equities funds averaged a negative return of -.12%.

Those top 30 mutual funds clearly outperformed the overall U.S. stock market, so guess which mutual funds were getting all the attention and being promoted in 2012? Yes, the same 30 mutual funds.

An investor may feel that they are making a prudent investment decision by choosing mutual funds that have had a successful five-year track-record. Now that we can look back, did those same 30 mutual funds outperform the overall U.S. market over the *next* five years?

No, they did not. From 2012 through 2016, those same 30 equity mutual funds had an average annual return of +4.35% while the average of all equity mutual funds averaged +12.04%, and the S&P 500 averaged +14.66% in the same period.[7] These Fund Managers did not repeat their performance, and by the time an investor figures out that their mutual funds are underperforming, they've already missed the growth experienced by the markets.

Year	2007–11	2012–16
Top 30 US Equity Funds Average Annual Return	5.07%	4.35%
All US Equity Funds Average Annual Return	-0.12%	12.04%
S&P 500 Average Annual Return	-0.25%	14.66%

---

7   Mutual fund data provided by CRSP Survivor Bias-Free Mutual Fund Database, includes funds that are U.S. Equity mutual funds. The S&P data are provided by Standard & Poor's Index Services Group. CRSP data provided by the Center for Research in Security Prices, University of Chicago. Indices are not available for direct investment; therefore, their performance does not reflect the expenses associated with the management of an actual portfolio. Past performance is not a guarantee of future results. Not actual investor results.

Bottom line: A fund manager's ability to pick stocks in the past has little to no correlation to his/her ability to do so consistently in the future.

MARKET TIMING

Market timing is any attempt to alter or change the mix of assets in a portfolio based on a prediction or forecast about the future. Someone who is trying to *time* the market attempts to "get out" *before* the market goes down, then "get back in" *before* the markets turn around and move up. There are many problems with this speculative behavior, and the basic *rules* of prudent investing are broken. When a market-timer sells out of the market, he or she no longer owns equities (where expected growth comes from), and they are no longer diversified—they hold cash. The markets are just as likely to surge in value right after this investor got out, causing them to lose out on growth. The markets are random and unpredictable in the short-term and often will not move in the direction the market-timer is predicting.

Even those who do not identify themselves as a market-timer are tempted to do just that when emotions like fear enter the picture. There always seems to be drama in the media about the stock markets. They are quick and consistent in their fear generating headlines like "The market's 'fear index' has exploded upward as stocks around the world plummet" (Business Insider, October 11, 2018), and favorite words such as "Panic," "Bloodbath," and "Plunge." Talking heads of the media may say something like, "It's time to get out of the market."

That should be warning enough—not to take free advice from the media. This is called market-timing. (For a deeper dive into understanding the perils of market timing, look online for the Forbes' article on "The Myth of Market Timing": https://www.forbes.com/sites/simonmoore/2016/03/07/the-myth-of-market-timing/)

> *"The evidence on investment managers' success with market timing is impressive—and overwhelmingly negative."*
> **Charles D. Ellis**

✎ PUTTING IT INTO PRACTICE

Can you remember a time when it was suggested to you that you buy, or invest in, something that later was revealed not to be a sound investment?

One of the best ways to avoid speculating and gambling with your money is to have a written investment policy statement; a plan that spells out your dos and don'ts in advance. Look at health as an example. If someone wanted to lose weight, and some inches around the waistline, they would do well to have written goals; a list of foods to eat, and foods to avoid, as well as scheduling exercise. When temptations arise, they can remind themselves of their plan (and hopefully flee temptation).

When market values drop, investors can easily react emotionally. Much more destructive than eating ice cream when stressed, getting out of the market when it is down can devastate wealth. You can refer to your written plan and be reminded that when market values drop, you buy more, or at minimum, stay disciplined through the downturn.

If you have an Investment Advisor, he or she can help you establish your personalized investment policy statement. As a starting point, you can begin with the outline on the next page.

My primary objective in investing is: preserve capital/growth of capital?

_____

_____

_____

My second objective in investing is: preserve capital/growth of capital?

_____

_____

_____

I will invest for _____ years.

I understand that market fluctuations are part of the normal market cycle, and when values are down, I will

_____.

I will be long-term minded because _like the weather, the average long-term experience in investing is never surprising, but the short-term experience constantly surprising._[1]

---

1   Ellis, Charles, _Winning the Loser's Game_

CHAPTER TEN

MEASURING SUCCESS OR FAILURE

MULTIPLY

"I have suffered losses," Abdiel lamented, "yet I have been blessed with many gains."

"I have learned the value of Solomon's words, 'Cast thy bread upon the waters,' and I have reaped abundance." "I will not let fear be my guide but will remain diligent in my pursuits. My lord will return one day, and I believe he will be pleased with my trading."

A STUDENT STUDIES for an exam and scores a B+; he can feel that he succeeded in taking that exam. A student who scored an F has failed that exam. Grades in school are a pretty simple system of measuring success or failure of a test, and the results come fairly quickly—the students are not kept in suspense very long before receiving their results.

Seeing that prudent investing is a long-term discipline, when and how do we measure success or failure? Will an instructor hand out our grade every three months, causing us anxiety as we await the results? No. Will there be a grading system with an "A" meaning success, and an "F" meaning failure? Again, the answer is no.

You will, however, see fluctuations in the value of your portfolio; rising values, and dropping values. And this is where the measurement system is vastly different from school. Up does not necessarily mean success, and down does not necessarily imply failure, and that's great news!

On a traditional report card, there is another measurement which parents are very interested in, and the student likes to ignore—and that is citizenship. Citizenship reports the student's classroom behavior during a period of time, as observed by the teacher. Johnny may well have earned high marks in his subjects, but if he has low citizenship scores, mom and dad are going to "have a talk" with Johnny, and he's not going to like it!

In a properly diversified portfolio, it is not so much the portfolio that receives the *citizenship* grade but rather the investor's behavior that should be evaluated. Markets move up as well as down. What was the investor's behavior during times of volatility? Did they respond emotionally, selling their investments when values dropped? Did they abandon their carefully crafted long-term investment strategy? Much worse than a low citizenship grade is the financial loss realized from irrational behavior.

Let's say Sam has a portfolio broadly diversified across the different asset classes, and a small portion in fixed income. He is forty years old, loves his occupation, and plans on continuing to work for another twenty years or more. The balance in his retirement account has grown to $80,000 over the past few relatively calm years in the market—he can get used to this! But then he hears on the news that a certain "Northern" country is ready to launch missiles. The media declares that war is imminent, and the pundits preach that everyone should "get out of the market" and wait until it is safer to invest. News headlines read "Stock selloff intensifies as fear begins to grip Wall St."[1]

Sam notices the market numbers are in the red and logs on to his retirement account to assess the damage. His account balance is now $65,670. He fears it is going to get worse before it gets better, believes the media's message and sells his holdings, moving to cash in order to *wait out the storm*. Not long after this media storm of doom and gloom, the markets rebound and grow to higher levels. Sam not only actualized a loss of almost $15,000, but he missed the growth that followed the temporary downturn.

---

1   Yahoo Finance, August 10, 2017

Sam would score an F in behavior. He broke the rules of prudent investing: He sold low (instead of selling when values are high); he no longer owns equities (which produce wealth over time), he is no longer diversified (he only holds cash), and he reacted on emotion rather than reason.

Paula also has a sizable amount in her 401(k). She also heard "the news" and saw the red numbers online, indicating a drop in the markets. Unlike Sam, Paula remembers the coaching from her investment advisor, teaching her that market ups and downs are all part of the nature of investing and that it is not the markets that devastate wealth, it is investor behavior.

Recalling one of the simple rules of investing, "Buy low, sell high," Paula presses on through the downturn, investing faithfully with each paycheck into her long-term retirement account. Not long after the media proclaim the "horror," market levels recover and are even a little higher than they were before the downturn. Paula, because of her discipline, was able to buy more shares of the funds she owns within her 401(k) at lower prices while they were down, and those share prices increased when the markets increased. Paula not only avoided losses during that time but profited through purchasing her investments on *sale*. Paula scores an A in investor's behavior.

HISTORICALLY, MARKET HIGHS FAR EXCEED MARKET LOWS

I will be the first to admit that it is not fun to be in the midst of a market downturn. This is where one's perspective can make or break the success in their portfolio. If we have a short-term point of view, fear can set in as we tend to think, "This is it! The collapse is coming," and then proceed to make decisions that will hurt our finances—selling at a loss. However, if we maintain a long-term point of view, remembering that market downturns are temporary, and that market recovery historically is much higher than the downturns, we can stay disciplined, avoid unnecessary losses and benefit from the coming upturn.

As an example, consider the behavior of the S&P 500 during the housing/credit crisis of 2008-2009:

2008	-38% (approximately)
3/2009–12/2015	296% (approximately)

During this time, if an investor panicked and sold their funds (in the S&P 500), not only would they have experienced a real loss as they got *out* of the market, they lost out on the huge growth that occurred during the next nine years. Granted, some investors may have gotten back into the market, but emotional investors generally wait until it is "safe" to get back in, meaning the markets have already recovered—and they still would have missed out on tremendous growth.

During the Dot-Com bubble of the early 2000s, we saw similar market behavior in the S&P 500:

2000–2002	-37.4%
2003–2007	81.7%

Again, those who give in to emotion and sell when values are down experience real losses and miss out on the growth that follows—if they are *out* of the market.

It is important to note that in the above examples, the market movement of only one investment category—the S&P 500—is measured. A properly diversified portfolio would only have a *portion* of their portfolio allocated to the S&P 500. Diversifying across several investment categories helps reduce the downside volatility as you can see above.

It is also helpful to know *real world* worst-case scenarios so that we can stay disciplined and be rewarded during times of volatility. When markets start to decline, how bad can it really get? Another way to ask that question is, if a portfolio has experienced a gain of 296% (as mentioned above), how much of a downturn will it take to wipe out all that growth? After all, that is what an investor is really concerned about, *will I lose my money?*

The answer is 70%. It would take a downturn of about 70% to bring the portfolio value back down to the level it was at before the 296% growth. While that is not impossible, it is not *likely*. The greatest recorded downturn in the US stock market occurred in 1929 and lasted through 1932, resulting in a decrease in value of -64%.

Consider the chart on the following page. The "Annualized Capital Return" percentage you see is the growth of that particular investment category over the years which *include* years of downturn. Through the *Great Crash of '29*, the Nixon-Watergate years of '73-'74, the Dot-Com bust of '00-'02, and the Credit Crisis of '08-'09—through all the downturns, the market still produced very favorable growth rates. (The US did not start tracking international stocks until the early 1970s)

Annualized Capital Return		
U.S. Micro Cap Stocks	12.38%	1927-2016
S&P 500 (Large US)	10.02%	1927-2016
Small Cap Value	14.92%	1927-2016
Large Value	12.03%	1927-2016
International Small	14.24%	1970-2016
International Large	9.28%	1970-2016

As we invest over the course of many years, staying disciplined to avoid emotional actions of getting in and out of the market, the "ups and downs" will level out to positive averages. Failure then would be measured by knowingly giving in to emotions and selling at a loss. Success would be measured by having stayed disciplined to your long-term investment strategy, soldiering through many seasons of ups and downs, and reaping the rewards of market growth.

PUTTING IT INTO PRACTICE

It is said that during times of volatility, wealth transfers from the fearful to the disciplined. Downturns occur, and diligent investors should expect them, and respond accordingly, either through buying more shares (on sale) or soldiering through, staying disciplined.

Once you put your written investment plan into place, come back to this page and write a note (while you are in a calm state of mind) **to your "future" self, reminding yourself what your plan is during seasons of downturns.**

_____

_____

_____

_____

_____

_____

When the markets decline, and I see values drop, I will ____?

_____

_____

_____

_____

_____

_____

CHAPTER ELEVEN

REASONS WE DO NOT INVEST

But he that had received one went and digged in
the earth, and hid his lord's money.

Matthew 25:18

MULTIPLY

It was an inquisitive thing, Abdiel thought to himself, that he never saw Tanel in the marketplace. Each evening when he would return to the great house, Taneli was always somewhere on the property. One Sabbath day, while Taneli was reclining in the great room surrounded by wonderful pillows and carpets, Abdiel offered his assistance:

"Why don't you come with me to the market tomorrow? I will introduce you to some merchant friends of mine."

"Thank you, but I have work to do on the grounds. You may work with your mind and words, but I work with my hands," Taneli replied, holding up his hands as if on exhibit.

"I believe you can benefit greatly from the trade with Lebanon and Egypt. The offer remains should you change your mind," Abdiel offered as he walked out of the room.

Taneli wrestled with many conflicting thoughts. *What do I know about trading? Why even try? What's the point? I know all about the vines and when to prune them. I will continue in their care.*

WHILE WE MAY NOT subscribe to the business acumen of the unfaithful steward, assuring ourselves that we would be better stewards, there are still many hindrances that we allow to keep us from saving and investing for the future.

OBSTACLES THAT KEEP US FROM INVESTING

According to the Federal Reserve's Report on the Economic Well-Being of U.S. Households in 2014, 47% of households indicate that they would have great difficulty handing an unexpected $400 expense.[1]

No one likes unexpected expenses. There are plenty of other ways we could enjoy that money. But this report points to a heavier matter. If so many households are unprepared for such a modest expense (compared to a $2,800 furnace, for example), where do we stand in our preparation for the future? All too often, we do not consider the source of future income to meet our needs ten, twenty, even thirty years from now.

Many deterrents can keep us from investing in our family's future.

TIME

Time is a deterrent that seems to be the most prominent. I *don't have the spare time to try and learn about investing; there are more important matters that require my full attention.* We also tend to focus on the financial concerns of today. There seems to be more than enough issues screaming for our

---

1   https://www.cnsnews.com/news/article/eric-scheiner/nearly-half-us-cant-afford-unexpected-400-bill-forgo-medical-treatment

attention *today*. If there were 30 hours in a day, some of us would still feel overwhelmed.

While the concern for present matters is important, we must not let the cares of today dominate our thoughts, attention, and thus, our actions. Doing so keeps us in "reactive" mode, tackling one current "need" and then the next. We suppress thoughts of our future needs, telling ourselves we'll address them when we finally have some free *time*.

We give our time to the things and persons we value in life. Sometimes, we allow our time to be hijacked. Social media is a prime example. We may have good intentions to simply log in quickly, check for updates, and maybe post something of interest, and may end up wondering how an hour has passed so quickly.

As of June 2018, Facebook users spent 58 minutes per day on the Facebook app and 53 minutes per day on Instagram.[2] The average college course is taught in 50 minutes, three days per week, over a period of thirteen weeks. Imagine what can be learned in a year, in place of so much time spent on social media?

For many of us, a decade or two will pass, and then we realize that we are not twenty anymore. Knowing that no plan for saving and investing for the future has been implemented, we get frustrated, and that frustration can prompt two different responses.

---

2   https://www.recode.net/2018/6/25/17501224/instagram-facebook-snapchat-time-spent-growth-data

One is that we get motivated to finally *start* saving and investing—because we are not getting any younger and we acknowledge that we have less time to prepare for our *older age*. The second is that we allow frustration with ourselves to prohibit us from moving forward. We tell ourselves, *I'm just not a saver*, or, *Well, it's too late to make a difference now*. If the Lord has given you the ability to earn an income today, you can find a way to start saving or investing.

NOT ENOUGH MONEY

Many believe they simply do not have the resources to start investing. Often, households suffer financial "Death by a thousand cuts."[3] It's not the large purchase that kills the household budget; it's the little expense—the little monthly bills that are added without thought or consideration of their impact on the family's financial health.

On how many platforms do we pay to view TV streaming? How many phone lines? How many online subscriptions, and Amazon purchases? A very eye-opening exercise (which can lead to recapturing dollars that are escaping) is to carefully look at every financial transaction in your bank account, over the past three months. Grab a highlighter and highlight transactions in the same category; shopping, eating out, entertainment, monthly subscriptions, etc. Add up these items to determine your monthly average. With this knowledge, you can be proactive in *choosing* how much you actually want to

---

3   https://www.investopedia.com/terms/d/death-1000-cuts.asp

spend, often reducing monthly amounts and re-directing those newfound dollars to saving and investing.

Some may view the amount they are able to invest as insignificant or *not nearly enough to make an impact.* Again, this can lead to putting off investing, with the thought that they will start investing later when they are making more money. As often happens, when our income does increase, we allow our expenses and lifestyle to increase as well. *Now that we're making more money, we can get that gym membership, buy that car on payments, increase the internet speed…*and the list goes on.

MISCONCEPTIONS

Some people struggle with the belief that *they* could actually accumulate a large sum of money for the future. To even mention $500,000 or $1,000,000 seems unattainable or *other-worldly* to them. But great things can happen when you combine discipline, consistency, and time. A twenty-year-old can prudently invest $100 per month and accumulate over $1 million by age 65. It is possible for thirty-year-old to reach $1 million investing $250 per month (prudently diversified and remaining disciplined) by age 65. A forty-year-old would need to invest about $750 per month to accomplish the same. Accumulating a respectable sum over time can be a reality.

Another broadly held misconception is that investing is an activity that causes people to lose all of their money! *It's a dangerous game that only the pros can play,* yet it is estimated that the baby-boomer has accumulated well over $68 trillion in retirement assets in the markets.

WE ARE COMFORTABLE WITH THE "HERE AND NOW"

For many families, it is enough just to keep up with the financial demands of today. "*Sufficient* unto *the* day is *the evil* thereof," so we live for today. We receive our paycheck and immediately tackle the items screaming for our dollars, today. The kids need clothes that actually fit them, sports uniforms are needed, as are braces. *We can't live* without the internet, so we need to pay for that service; we want some form of television programming—so we pay for that, and who can function without a smartphone? Plus, we have to enjoy life a little, right? There are vacations to plan, gifts to buy, new restaurants to experience, and grab our go-to coffee drink. Then one day, we wake up and realize we are not twenty anymore, and we're way behind in this investing for the future business! It's easy to get stuck managing for today only.

PROCRASTINATION

I took a Macro Economics class while in college, and one of the principles I heard taught was *opportunity cost*. Opportunity cost is making one choice over another and missing out on the benefit of the forgone choice. If I were to spend $50 on an item that caught my eye on Amazon, I would not have that $50 to invest and enjoy the compounding growth on that investment over many years.

I cannot say I *learned* that principle at age eighteen. It would take me decades before I learned the value of pausing and considering the opportunity cost of the dollars I decided to spend before I spent them. There are countless ways to spend money that bring us immediate enjoyment. I'm sure you've discovered at some point that you can't simply use your income for enjoyment—there are some responsibilities in life to tend to.

The temptation to put off investing today's dollars for tomorrow's benefit is powerful, because often, we do not stop to consider the opportunity cost—the benefit of these dollars working for us in the future, over today's enjoyment. So, we put off investing, telling ourselves we will *get to it later*. Solomon warns, "In all labour there is profit: but the talk of the lips tendeth only to penury" (Proverbs 14:23).

Dan Ariely, James B. Duke Professor of Psychology and Behavioral Economics at Duke University, writes: *When we promise to save our money, we are in a cool state. When we promise to exercise and watch our diet, again we're cool. But then the lava flow of hot emotion comes rushing in: just when we promise to save, we see a new car, a mountain bike, or a pair of shoes that we must have. Just when we plan to exercise regularly, we find a reason to sit all day in front of the television. And as for the diet? I'll take that slice of chocolate cake and begin the diet in earnest tomorrow. Giving up on our long-term goals for immediate gratification, my friend, is procrastination.*[4]

---

4   Ariely, Dan. *Predictably Irrational,* Revised and expanded edition, Harper Collins 2009, pg141

WE SPEND

Benjamin Franklin said, "Beware of little expenses; a small leak will sink a great ship." We definitely live in an exciting age. Innovation has brought the world closer to us. From the comfort of our homes, we have the world markets available to us at our fingertips. With a few strokes of the keys, we can order a coffee mug to add to our collection on a Sunday and have it delivered to our doorstep on Monday. We can obtain nearly anything our hearts desire so quickly and easily.

The reality is, we like *stuff*. Americans have three times the space than we had fifty years ago, yet we spend $24 billion each year to store our stuff. Consumerism permeates our culture, and it is effortless to get caught up in what some call the h*edonic treadmill*, which is the increase of expectations and desires as one's income rises. The tendency is to buy more things, and to take on additional bills as we make more money, leaving us with less margin, or disposable income.

One survey, by the Bureau of Labor Statistics, found that Americans spend more than 90% of income. The next generation smartphone gets released, and we *need* its faster processing and additional features. Not having the $800 to purchase the new phone, we simply add it to cell service plan, and our monthly payments increase by *only* $30 per month. If we want to watch a TV program without commercials—no problem, for just $12 a month, we can binge watch all we want. Satellite radio for cars, *just* $13 a month— and the bills keep creeping up until we get to the point where we wonder, *why don't I have any money?*

WE OBLIGATE GOD TO TAKE CARE OF OUR FINANCIAL FUTURE

The just shall live by faith. This truth is stated four times in Scripture. In many areas of our lives, we tend to lean on faith alone, without action on our part.

When it comes to thinking about our financial needs in the distant future, we tend to think; *God will take care of me.* To an extent, that is true; according to Matthew 6:33, if we seek first the kingdom of God and seek His righteousness (seeking to live righteously), then "all these things shall be added unto you." The "things" alluded to in this portion of Scripture are food, clothing, and shelter—these were the issues that Christ's followers were worried about.

Consider the financial needs of today: food, shelter, and clothing. When we *seek first the kingdom of God and His righteousness* (our part, by faith), God does His part and provides for us. Consider the source of your income today. It is very likely that you sought the Lord to help and guide you as to where you would work. A job interview most likely was conducted during which you presented yourself, your qualifications, and ability to perform the work required. It is also likely that you had to prepare for the area of work you applied for, perhaps a college degree, or past experience at other employers. To gain such experience, you had to work and learn and put forth effort and discipline. Thus, there has been concentrated effort on your part to obtain today's income. It is God that gives us the ability to work and earn a living (Deuteronomy 8:18), and it is God who answers prayer and guides us—and it is we who *labor*.

If such effort is made to obtain and maintain *today's* source of income, by faith, how would planning and putting forth effort for our future source of income be any different? God has given us minds to think and reason, and His Word to guide us. We can know that, should the Lord tarry His return, these bodies of flesh age, deteriorate, and are prone to illness and injury. There likely would come a day when we can no longer perform our usual duties in earning an income and would need to draw an income from another source—our savings and investments. Social security *might* be there for you, but it was designed and implemented as a means to keep you from starving—not to meet all your financial needs in retirement or disability.

THE CHALLENGE

I want to encourage you to determine to take care of your family and yourself by planning for your financial future. Most likely, you are working hard to earn today's income, providing for today's needs of your family. Think 5, 10, even 20 years down the road, should the Lord tarry His return, you will still need income; saving and investing are the more effective means to prepare for such time.

In the process of living for today, we do not want to sacrifice *tomorrow*. We can find a balance between enjoying what our money can do for us today, and what it can do for us later in life, trusting in the Lord all along the way.

We have no problems spending money in areas that bring us pleasure or satisfaction, and areas we deem as *important*. Simply make the mental switch to viewing saving and investing as a priority and you'll be able to recapture previously misdirected dollars.

📝 PUTTING IT INTO PRACTICE

Can you identify one or more obstacles keeping you back from investing as you should? List them here:

_____

_____

_____

_____

_____

_____

_____

Given your obstacle(s), what steps will you take to overcome your own objections?

_____

_____

_____

_____

_____

_____

_____

_____

_____

CHAPTER TWELVE

HOW LONG SHOULD
WE INVEST?

*After a long time, the lord of those servants
cometh, and reckoneth with them.*

Matthew 25:19

MULTIPLY

Many seasons had come and gone since his lord's departure and Abdiel maintained his resolve to please him in the management of his wealth. Although his children had grown into adults during his lord's absence, time seemed to have passed like the twinkling of an eye. It amazed Abdiel to consider all that he had learned over many years; from having no trading knowledge to enjoying great success, from painful losses to great fortunes. Now that he was older, he assigned the physical work of his trading to hired laborers, and labored with his mind, overseeing his many enterprises.

IT CAN EASILY SEEM that the faithful servants quickly *doubled* their master's money as verse 16 states, "Then he that had received the five talents went and traded with the same and made them other five talents." Boom! It was that easy. In as little as **one** verse, this faithful servant earned a 100% return on investment!

I don't want you to get too excited at the thought of doubling your money so quickly.

Jesus teaches that the lord of these servants returned "after a long time." How long is a *long time*? Many *seasons*, many years actually. In Joshua 24:7, we read, "…and ye dwelt in the wilderness a long season." The children of Israel dwelt in the wilderness for over forty years. We know that Christ, in teaching this parable of the talents, was preparing His followers to occupy during His *long* absence. Jesus ascended over 2000 years ago, which is a long *time*, and yet we are to love and look forward to His return (2 Timothy 4:8).

How do we apply this to the discipline of saving and investing?

We all have our own goals with their respective timelines. Generally speaking, investing to have a future income is a long-term endeavor. That's fantastic if you're 20, not so exciting if you are 55 and only now wish to start investing.

Time; how long investments are held, and the period in which investment performance can be measured, is a vital element in a successful investing plan. Investing is really a life-long discipline. Consider the thirty-year-old who starts investing $300 per month through age sixty-five. Earning an average of 8%, he would accumulate over $642,000.

A forty-year-old investor does the same, investing $300 every month through sixty-five, earning an average of 8% per year, and accumulates roughly $272,000.

That's a huge difference! Why the huge disparity between the two accumulated values? Time. It takes time, regular contributions, diversification, and discipline to accumulate wealth for your future.

The mindset that one can simply get in the market, score big and get out, is perilous not only to their financial health but to their emotional and physical health as well. Proverbs 28:20, 22 warns, "A faithful man shall abound with blessings: but he that maketh haste to be rich shall not be innocent," and "He that hasteth to be rich hath an evil eye, and considereth not that poverty shall come upon him."

Those who stay disciplined to keeping a properly diversified portfolio for a long period of time will notice that the performance of their investments (movements up and down) will start to move closer to an expected *average* annual rate of growth. In the short-term, the markets seem to behave like an emotional teenager, dramatically up or down from one moment to the next. But over a long period of time, those dramatic ups and downs actually level out to form an average anticipated annual rate of return. Just like the rain patterns on the East Coast may seem random to someone visiting for just a few days; when viewed over a longer period of time, it is quite normal and predictable.

HARVEST TIME

My mom has several fruit trees in her backyard. I just love summer fruit. My favorite is the Loquat fruit, and she has two of these trees; one is over 25 years old and the other is much younger. Every summer, I make a bee-line to the older Loquat tree because its fruit always seems to have a darker orange color and incredible sweetness! The fruit on the younger tree, while acceptable, tends to taste a bit sourer than those of the older tree. Then there is the Plum tree (and I so love Plums). At five years old, it still has not produced fruit sweet enough to enjoy.

Now, I am not an Arborist, and I'm confident that there is much to be said about the proper care and feeding of fruit trees, but what I do know is that her more mature trees produce the sweetest fruit. Time is Archimedes lever in investing. Archimedes is often quoted as saying, "Give me a lever long enough and a place to stand, and I can move the earth." In investing, that lever is time (and the place to stand, of course, is on a firm and realistic investment policy). [1]

After investing for decades, the time of harvest arrives— the time to enjoy the fruits of your labor and draw income (withdrawals) from your investment account(s).

---

1   Charles Ellis, *Winning the Loser's Game, Fifth Edition, Timeless Strategies for Successful Investing*, 2010 McGraw Hill

RETIREMENT; NOT THE END, BUT ANOTHER BEGINNING

Some may view retiring as the end of their investing experience, as if it's time to cash in, park the money in a bank, and take monthly withdrawals until the money runs out. I hope that retirement marks a new season for you. Think of all the possibilities. Some will travel to visit family; some will take missions trips, serve the Lord in new capacities or even write a book! (It's not too late to read Dr. Seuss' book, Oh the Places You'll Go! —My favorite).

It is estimated that the average American lives twenty years past retirement. You can bet that cost of food, fuel, and taxes will increase during those years. Because of this, it is important that your money maintains a level of growth to keep up with, or exceed, the rate of inflation. You will not necessarily need as much growth as you pursued in your younger years. At this point, preservation becomes a higher priority.

It is possible to structure your investment account(s) in such a way as to earn, for example, 5%, while you are withdrawing 4% per year as income—potentially maintaining your capital. This is often accomplished by reducing the portion of your investments in equities to 40%-50% and increasing fixed income (as a cushion) to 50%-60% (Consult with a licensed investment professional).

📝 PUTTING IT INTO PRACTICE

I have observed and counseled those whom I would consider successful investors, who did most of their accumulation through setting up an automatic investing schedule (like a 401(k)), then faithfully contribute throughout their working years, retiring 30-plus years later with over a million dollars. Have you identified a means by which you can invest automatically on a monthly basis?

_____

_____

_____

I have set up a plan with: _____

_____

_____

I am contributing $ _____ per _____

_____

_____

I can see myself continuing this for ____ years.

_____

_____

CHAPTER THIRTEEN

STAND AND GIVE
AN ACCOUNT

...the lord of those servants cometh, and
reckoneth with them.

Matthew 25:19

MULTIPLY

"Abdiel, it has been a very long time. Please, give an account of your stewardship," Yada said in a fatherly voice.

Abdiel could hardly contain his excitement. This was the day he had been waiting and praying for, for many years.

"Lord, thou deliveredst unto me five talents: behold, I have gained beside them five talents more."

A kind smile spread across Yada's face as he spoke the sweetest words to Abdiel's ears, "Well done, thou good and faithful servant: thou hast been faithful over a few things, I will make thee ruler over many things: enter thou into the joy of thy lord."

Hot tears streamed down Abdiel's face. His heart was so full of joy he could not control his sobbing. "Thank you, my lord," was all he could manage to reply.

I **AM IN NO WAY** equating doubling our investments as a qualification for pleasing our Lord. Ultimately, everything we do, in both words and deeds, should be done for the glory of God—this includes the stewarding of the financial resources He has entrusted to our care. During this life, there are certain built-in consequences for our actions. If we spend all of our income, we end up without savings, sometimes debt, and dependent upon others. If, on the other hand, we do our part in applying the biblical principles of saving and investing, while trusting in the Lord and not money, we can avoid indebtedness, dependence on others, and may be in a position to do more for the cause of Christ.

The parable of the talents is a story Jesus teaches to help us prepare for and anticipate His coming. He calls us to be faithful stewards of everything He has entrusted to us, knowing we will stand and give an account of our stewardship upon His return.

It takes some effort and imagination to picture yourself standing before Jesus Christ, God the Son; the One who loved you and delivered you from the law of sin and death. I believe we see in Scripture that God indeed wants us thinking about being with Him in His holy presence. God's Word directs us to "…seek those things which are above, where Christ sitteth on the right hand of God. Set your affection on the things above, not on things on the earth" (Colossians 3: 1b-2).

Have you given any thought lately to the Judgment Seat of Christ? I'm sure the term *judgment* does not have a cheerful ring to it, but oh, what an event it will be! Whether you face it, when your life on earth is over, or when we are all caught up together to be with Him, there will be an appointed time for each of us to stand before Christ and give an account of all that we have done with our lives.

"Ought not this to make us feel what an intense thing the Christian life is—not a thing of sleepiness or haphazard, not a thing to be left now and then to a little superficial consideration? It must be a matter which demands all our strength, so that when we are saved there is a living principle put within us which demands all our energies, and gives us energy over and above any that we ever had before. Those who dream that carelessness will find its way to heaven have made a great mistake."— Charles H Spurgeon

Paul reminds us in 2 Corinthians 5:10, "For we must all appear before the judgment seat of Christ; that every one may receive the things done in his body, according to that he hath done, whether it be good or bad." Why would the Bible say that we will give an account for the bad that we've done if we are in Heaven, and there is no sin, no bad, and no evil there?

First Corinthians chapter three provides some more details. As Paul teaches that we are laborers together with God, he teaches that the foundation of our labor for God is Jesus Christ.

Now if any man build upon this foundation gold, silver, precious stones, wood, hay, stubble; Every man's work shall be made manifest (known): for the day shall declare it, because it shall be revealed by fire; and the fire shall try every man's work of what sort it is. If any man's work abide which he hath built thereupon, he shall receive a reward. If any man's work shall be burned, he shall suffer loss: but he himself shall be saved; yet so as by **fire**. (1 Corinthians 3:12–15)

Did you notice how often the word *fire* was used? You see, heaven and earth will pass away (Revelation 21:1), and all worldly deeds will pass with it. The Judgment Seat of Christ is a time of receiving rewards for all we have done, in faith, for the Lord. There are different rewards for the various acts of service we have done.

Just to name a few, there are rewards for denying ourselves— Matthew 16:24–27; for generous giving—Matthew 6:20, and for enduring persecution—Luke 6:22–23. In many references to the rewards we will receive, the Greek word misthos is used, meaning "pay for services, hire, reward, wages." These are real, physical rewards!

Other rewards are: The opportunity to rule and reign with Christ during the Millennial reign based on our faithfulness (Matthew 25:21–23), and also the earning of *crowns* (Revelation 2:10; 1 Corinthians 9:24–25; Philippians 4:1; 1 Peter 5:1–4; and 2 Timothy 4:6-8).

The "gold, silver and precious stones" acts that we have done for the Lord will be rewarded. The "wood, hay and stubble"—those things we've done for ourselves with wrong motives—will burn, and we will lose those rewards. Think of it like an Olympian who trained, ran the race, and earned a medal, only to have the medal stripped away because it was "made known" that he used steroids; that athlete went through all the motions, but his *motive* was wrong—he acted selfishly.

Our race is being closely and lovingly monitored. We are called to be faithful stewards. Christ died for us, and it is only reasonable that we should live for Him. Even though we owe Him everything, He still delights in rewarding us for living faithfully for Him. We should long for the judgment seat of Christ rather than dread it. With your actions and affections today, are you storing up treasure? Earning rewards? Or are you potentially losing rewards? Determine today to live with eternity in mind. Second John 8 encourages us to "look to yourselves, that we lose not those things which we have wrought, but that we receive a *full reward*" (emphasis added).

MORALS-BASED INVESTING

People often ask me if a Christian investor can be broadly diversified in their investments and avoid immoral companies? I understand why they ask that question; they do not want to financially *support* companies who sell products or provide services that we are morally against.

In order to identify which companies we as Christians would label as immoral, we would ask such questions as: Do they sell alcohol? Do they sell pornography or Rated R movies? Do they support or perform abortions? Do they financially promote lifestyles that God says are sinful? Do they directly or indirectly financially support human trafficking?

It is relatively easy to filter out the obvious *offenders*, companies that make and sell alcohol, pornography companies, and Planned Parenthood. But it starts to get a little muddy when we look at retail stores for instance. What about your favorite, *good 'ole American superstore* (Wal-Mart, Target for example)? They sell alcohol, Rated R movies, and may financially support charitable causes, on a benevolent basis, that we are morally against.

What about your favorite hardware store, do they give money to Planned Parenthood, and charities that support lifestyles God teaches against? How about your cell phone service company? Do you know their corporate culture, core values, and philanthropic giving?

We could ask about the electric company, the make of vehicle you purchase, who makes your cereal, the list goes on ad nauseam.

The reality is that we live in a fallen world, and are surrounded by people who need the Lord, and it is next to impossible to limit our buying of goods and services to only morally sound companies.

This leads us to the necessity of defining what we mean by "financially supporting" these companies.

The thought is, if I own a few shares of XYZ company, I am financially supporting them. Let's talk about how you buy shares today and what, if anything, it means financially to the company itself.

Let's begin with an analogy. If you were interested in a book by a ministry leader whom you respect and purchase one of his books on E-bay or Thriftbooks, would you be financially supporting him? No. Why is that? You bought the book on the secondary market, from someone else who previously purchased the book. This ministry leader would receive no royalty payment from your purchase.

However, if you desired to support this ministry leader financially, you could send money straight to his ministry, usually through their website, or even purchase ministry resources straight through the ministry. These actions *do* financially support that ministry.

When you and I buy stocks, we do so through the secondary market. A brokerage house is generally employed to match your request to *buy* shares, with someone else's bid to *sell* their shares—the company itself makes no profit from your purchase of their stocks. They made their money when they initially offered their company for sale to the public through an Initial Public Offering (IPO), in which the major brokerage firms bought the often millions of shares offered, and we all get access to them *second hand*.

As you've read, it is not considered prudent investing to pick individual stocks as a long-term investment strategy. If you are globally and domestically diversified, it is very likely that your mutual or index funds may own several thousand different companies. Is there a chance that those funds may own a few companies who represent immorality? Yes. You own shares in a fund, whose value goes up or down based on the collective movement of all of the companies the fund owns.

The question is, does owning a share or two (more likely, partial shares) of a company within a mutual fund financially support that company? I submit that it does not.

What does financially support a company, unequivocally, is your *purchasing dollars*. When you spend $600 per month on groceries at the store of your choice, you are financially supporting them. If you choose, perhaps due to moral issues, to take that $600 per month and shop elsewhere, that will have a financial impact on that store. If dozens or even hundreds of Christians do their purchasing dollars elsewhere, that would indeed have a negative financial impact on that same store.

We support companies with our dollars. We have a greater financial impact on our purchases than we do with stock ownership.

Let's say you had $50,000 invested in three different mutual funds, and the total number of companies held in those funds were 3,000. There is a good chance that your favorite, globally recognized entertainment company is among those 3,000 companies.

That entertainment company has 1.9 billion shares out there in the world, trading at about $100 per share. It is complicated to do the math, but it may be that your portion of shares off that company may be one share, two shares, and in some cases, a fraction of a share. Does your fractional share, even 1 or 2 shares, impact the overall price of the 1.9 billion shares? No. However, does your consumption of that company's entertainment, plus food purchases, souvenirs, and annual pass purchases have an impact on their finances? Absolutely!

The bottom line is, if we don't want to support immoral companies financially, then we simply avoid using our money to purchase pornography, alcohol, drugs, abortions, etc.

ABOUT THE AUTHOR

Tim Rosen and his wife, Victoria, have been married over thirty-one years and have served together at Lancaster Baptist Church for over twenty years. Tim is a Registered Investment Advisor Representative and Founder of Faith and Finance Ministries which provides Christ-focused financial teaching throughout the United States as well as internationally. He also hosts the Faith and Finances Podcast.

ALSO AVAILABLE

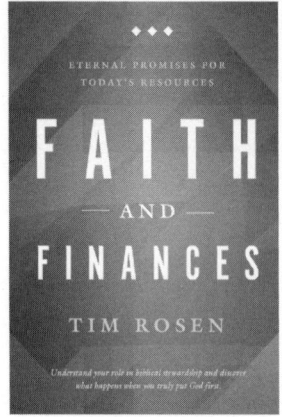

Faith and Finances
Eternal Promises for Today's Resources

Many Christians assume that money is a matter of budgets and spreadsheets, income and expenses. They think of it strictly in terms of material or emotional benefits and results.

But Scripture gives us a larger—an eternal—perspective. Woven throughout Scripture are principles and promises that deal with our finances—assurances that God will meet our needs and instructions for investing our resources into eternity.

In these pages, discover how you can trust and follow God's Word to teach, instruct, correct, comfort, and guide in this vital, and very personal area of life.

ALSO AVAILABLE

Against the Grain
Avoiding the Financial Pitfalls
of Conventional Wisdom

In the midst of today's ever-shifting finances, it is important to evaluate your financial goals as you progress through life. In these pages, you will explore the dangers of following conventional wisdom and be challenged to examine your own financial path in order to avoid potential pitfalls!

An Excellent Resource to Help...

- Couples and individuals plan for retirement
- Participants in employer-sponsored retirement plans avoid unnecessary taxes and losses
- Homeowners have financial balance and peace of mind
- Anyone who earns an income to get out of debt and accumulate wealth
- Those who are in debt conquer their money patterns

O'BRYANT & ASSOCIATES

To start your coaching experience, contact Nathan O'Bryant at 731-986-3445